DATE DUE

IMPLEMENTATION:
MAKING THINGS HAPPEN

Anita M. Pankake, Ed.D.

Professor of Educational Administration
Texas A & M University-Commerce
Commerce, Texas

EYE ON EDUCATION
6 DEPOT WAY WEST, SUITE 106
LARCHMONT, NY 10538
(914) 833–0551
(914) 833–0761 fax

ISBN 1-883-001-53-6

Library of Congress Cataloging-in-Publication Data
Pankake, Anita M., 1947–
    Implementation : making things happen / Anita M.Pankake.
        p.   cm. — (The school leadership library)
    Includes bibliographical references (p.).
    ISBN 1-883-001-53-6
    1. School management and organization—United States. 2. Educational
change—United States. 3. Educational leadership—United States.   I. Title.
II. Series.
LB2805.P32   1998
371.2—dc21   97-48822
                                                                       CIP

10 9 8 7 6 5 4 3 2 1

Editorial and production services provided by Richard H. Adin Freelance
Editorial Services, 9 Orchard Drive, Gardiner, NY 12525 (914-883-5884)

If you would like information about how to become a member of the **School Leadership Library**, please contact:

Eye On Education
6 Depot Way, Suite 106
Larchmont, NY 10538
Phone: (914) 833-0551
Fax: (914) 833-0761

FOREWORD

The School Leadership Library was designed to show practicing and aspiring principals what they should know and be able to do to be effective leaders of their schools. The books in this series were written to answer the question, "How can we improve our schools by improving the effectiveness of our principals?"

Success in the principalship, like in other professions, requires mastery of a knowledge and skills base. One of the goals of the National Policy Board for Educational Administration (sponsored by NAESP, NASSP, AASA, ASCD, NCPEA, UCEA, and other professional organizations) was to define and organize that knowledge and skill base. The result of our efforts was the development of a set of 21 "domains," building blocks representing the core understanding and capabilities required of successful principals.

The 21 domains of knowledge and skills are organized under four broad areas: Functional, Programmatic, Interpersonal, and Contextual. They are as follows:

FUNCTIONAL DOMAINS

Leadership
Information Collection
Problem Analysis
Judgment
Organizational Oversight
Implementation
Delegation

PROGRAMMATIC DOMAINS

Instruction and the Learning
    Environment
Curriculum Design
Student Guidance and
    Development
Staff Development
Measurement and Evaluation
Resource Allocation

INTERPERSONAL DOMAINS

Motivating Others
Interpersonal Sensitivity
Oral and Nonverbal Expression
Written Expression

CONTEXTUAL DOMAINS

Philosophical and Cultural
    Values
Legal and Regulatory
    Applications
Policy and Political Influences
Public Relations

These domains are not discrete, separate entities. Rather, they evolved only for the purpose of providing manageable descriptions of essential content and practice so as to better understand the entire complex role of the principalship. Because human behavior comes in "bunches" rather than neat packages, they are also overlapping pieces of a complex puzzle. Consider the domains as converging streams of behavior that spill over one another's banks but that all contribute to the total reservoir of knowledge and skills required of today's principals.

The School Leadership Library was established by General Editors David Erlandson and Al Wilson to provide a broad examination of the content and skills in all of the domains. The authors of each volume in this series offer concrete and realistic illustrations and examples, along with reflective exercises. You will find their work to be of exceptional merit, illustrating with insight the depth and interconnectedness of the domains. This series provides the fullest, most contemporary, and most useful information available for the preparation and professional development of principals.

Scott Thomson
Executive Secretary
National Policy Board for
Educational Administration

PREFACE

In *Principals for Our Changing Schools: The Knowledge and Skill Base*, Scott Thomson describes the 21 Performance Domains of principal performance as "...converging streams of behavior that spill over onto one another's banks but that all contribute to the total reservoir of knowledge and skills required of today's principals." The metaphor works well to emphasize that the separate skills are not discrete and should separately be considered for their particular contributions to the blend of behaviors that constitute exemplary principal performance. In this book, Anita Pankake extends the metaphor to state that the Implementation domain serves as the riverbed into which the converging streams of the other 20 domains flow and gives shape and meaning to them. Her point is well taken. Until knowledge and skill result in implementation in the school setting, they have no defined impact on the educational process. As is demonstrated throughout this book, excellent plans and intentions often fail at the implementation stage.

In her discussion of this key domain, Dr. Pankake closely follows the definition provided by the National Policy Board for Educational Administration:

> Making things happen; putting programs and change efforts into action; facilitating coordination and collaboration of tasks; establishing project checkpoints and monitoring progress; providing "midcourse" corrections when actual outcomes start to diverge from intended outcomes or when new conditions require adaptation; supporting those responsible for carrying out projects and plans.

The various elements of this definition are explored in the chapters that follow and are clearly linked to the other elements of the definition. Each element is supported with school-based examples and with many practical tools for applying the principles that underlie it. Practical exercises at the end of each chapter give the principal guidance and direction for developing implementation skills.

Chapters 2 through 4 describe the principles and procedures that underlie implementation. Chapter 2 looks at what principals have to make happen and provides a useful scheme for classifying implementation situations: routine, new (nonroutine), and unique. Chapter 3 provides some excellent models for carefully planning and managing the implementation process. Chapter 4 speaks to those skills that are required for facilitating the coordination and collaboration of tasks.

Chapter 5 addresses the important but often neglected function of monitoring implementation. It explains a procedure that will allow the principal to focus monitoring in an efficient and effective manner by expertly shifting from scanning to focusing to probing activities, depending upon the changing characteristics of the activities being monitored.

While the principal is responsible for implementation, the principal is usually not the one who is actually doing it. The principal depends upon a wide variety of other people—teachers, counselors, students, parents, and others—to make things happen. Chapter 6 emphasizes the importance of supporting those responsible for implementation, whether by providing staff development and professional growth opportunities, providing a supportive collegial network, or facilitating removal of organizational barriers.

This is an extremely practical book for the principal. It is methodical in its presentation and clear in its message: Implement! Make it happen now!

David A. Erlandson
Alfred P. Wilson

ABOUT THE AUTHOR

Dr. Anita M. Pankake, a former teacher, team leader, assistant principal, and principal, is currently a Professor of Educational Administration at Texas A & M University–Commerce. Dr. Pankake holds an undergraduate and a master's degree from Indiana State University, Terre Haute, Indiana, and her doctorate from Loyola University–Chicago. She has published in the *Journal of Staff Development, Educational Considerations, People and Education, NASSP Bulletin, Educational Horizons,* and other professional journals. She has given numerous speeches and presented a variety of workshops focused on change and school improvement issues. She is an active member of several national professional associations including Association for Supervision and Curriculum Development and the National Staff Development Council and she is a member of the governing boards for the Texas Staff Development Council and the Texas Council of Women School Executives.

ACKNOWLEDGMENTS

So many individuals deserve thanks for the various types of assistance given during the development and implementation of this writing project. First, my thanks go to Dr. Alfred P. Wilson who invited me to become a part of the Leadership Library authors. This was a wonderful continuation of the mentoring he so generously provided when we worked together at Kansas State University. Once a part of the project, I was provided an opportunity to know Dr. David Erlandson. Dr. Erlandson served as my editorial contact as the work developed. I must comment on Dr. Erlandson's patience and gentle coaching manner as he moved me forward with his positive and productive feedback over these several months. Thank you Dave. Also, my thanks go to Ms. Cynthia Hibbitts, Assistant Principal in Garland ISD, who was kind enough to read this manuscript for content and technical suggestions.

Many colleagues and friends here at Texas A & M University–Commerce were important in monitoring my progress toward the completion of this project also. Dr. David P. Thompson and Dr. Gwen Schroth were of particular influence with their "How's the book coming?" inquiries. My dearest of friends, Dr. Rita Cook in Salina, Kansas, and Mrs. Anna Marie Lamb of Naperville, Illinois, both provided subtle support via their steady requests for a copy of the book whenever it was completed. Now I can give them their copies with my thanks for the faith they had in me on this project and many others over the years we have known each other. I look forward to further adventures with each of them.

Most importantly in these acknowledgments is my indebtedness to my husband, Dr. David W. Pankake. This book is dedicated to him. He is, without question, "the wind beneath my wings"; he has been, and will be forever, my most admired educator, my mentor, and my model for life-long learning. There would be no completed book without his willingness to read and edit, to discuss ideas, and to offer his wisdom. Each and every day that I am allowed to be in his world and to have him in mine I count as my good fortune.

TABLE OF CONTENTS

1

AN INTRODUCTION TO IMPLEMENTATION

In 1993, the National Policy Board for Educational Administration published *Principals for Our Changing Schools: The Knowledge and Skill Base*. This document describes, in detail, a knowledge and skill base for the principalship organized into 21 domains. The 21 domains make up a core of things that individuals need to know about and be able to do in fulfilling the role of principal. The NPBEA emphasizes that while the domains form a convenient way of sorting and categorizing the knowledge and skills, the domains are not discrete from one another, but instead are "overlapping pieces of a complex puzzle." The NPBEA identified implementation as one of the 21 domains of essential knowledge and skills needed by principals. Implementation is one of seven categories that the NPBEA grouped under the heading of "Functional Domains." Functional Domains are those that "address the organizational processes and techniques by which the mission of the school is achieved. They provide for the educational program to be realized and allow the institution to function." This book is about implementation. It is about what implementation means, how implementation happens, and the knowledge and skills principals need to be quality implementers. Cuban gives voice to some feelings common in the experience of many educators:

> In such a decentralized yet national system of schooling that encourages plural interest groups and much prodding of professionals to alter what they do, it should come as no surprise that many reforms seldom go beyond getting adopted as policy. Most get implemented in word rather than deed, especially in classrooms. What often ends up in districts and schools are

1

signs of reform in new rules, different tests, revised organizational charts, and new equipment. Seldom are
the deepest structures of schooling that are embedded
in the school's use of time and space, teaching practices, and classroom routines fundamentally altered
even at those historical moments when reforms seek
those alterations as the goal....Why? (Cuban, 1990,
p. 9)

The history of educational change initiatives is crowded,
while the history of successful implementation of these initiatives is less so. The frustration of being poised to implement a
much needed or desired change only to have the agenda
switched or the efforts blocked or dropped is an experience
common to veteran educators at all levels. Knowledge about
why this happens and has happened so consistently in the past
can be helpful in understanding how future attempts to implement changes can be more successful. Implementing change
initiatives, however, is a rather traditional and narrow view of
this domain of knowledge and skills. The inference is a restrictive one; that is, that knowledge and skills regarding implementation are needed only when change is desired. However,
knowledge and skills of implementation are needed daily in
myriad ways in schools and school districts. Implementation
should be viewed as the riverbed into which the "converging
streams of behavior" from the other 20 knowledge and skill domains run and as evidenced within the schools and in the behavior of children they serve. This more broad, less restrictive
view provides the framework for this book. Focusing carefully
on what we currently know about implementation in all its
forms can assist practitioners in becoming more effective implementers. While others may talk and/or write about implementing, school administrators and classroom teachers are expected to "make it happen," that is, to implement. That is the
central theme of this work. In the remaining pages of this Introduction, implementation is defined and an explanation of a
broader perspective of implementation is presented. Additionally, an overview of the contents for each of the remaining
chapters is provided and a concluding statement regarding implementation's place within and among NPBEA's 21 domains
is offered.

IMPLEMENTATION DEFINED

The National Policy Board for Educational Administration uses numerous phrases and synonyms to define the implementation domain such as, "making things happen; putting programs and change efforts into action; facilitating coordination and collaboration of tasks; establishing project checkpoints and monitoring progress; providing 'midcourse' corrections when actual outcomes start to diverge from intended outcomes or when new conditions require adaptation; and, supporting those responsible for carrying out projects and plans." Another source for defining "implementation" is *The American Heritage Dictionary (Second College Edition)*. It lists the term "implementation" as a form of the word "implement." "Implement" can be both a noun and a verb. As a noun, "implement" implies "means employed to achieve a given end; agent." As a verb, "implement" means "to put into practical effect; carry out." These "means to an end" and activity-oriented definitions connect well with the NPBEA description of the implementation domain. Additionally, they enhance an understanding of implementation by identifying it as both a noun and a verb. This grammatical perspective infers that implementation has both product and process dimensions. Implementation involves the what (a state or destination desired) and the how (strategies for making the journey to that state or destination). It has both an activity and an accomplishment dimension. This dual role contributes to the breadth and complexity of the knowledge and skills needed for implementation. Additionally, it signals the extent to which elements of the other 20 domains may be embedded in the implementation domain and how elements from implementation may surface in other domains.

AN OVERVIEW OF THIS VOLUME ON IMPLEMENTATION

In developing this volume of the School Leadership Library series, many of the terms and phrases found in the NPBEA's definition of implementation are used as chapter headings. Every attempt has been made to align the content of this volume with the intent of the NPBEA and perhaps to go beyond that intent. This overview is intended to give the reader a sense of what lies ahead. Chapter 2, "Making Things Happen," includes an overview of what principals have to make happen, how these responsibilities might be categorized, and some necessary conditions for making things happen. Chapter 3, "Putting Programs and Change Efforts Into Action," focuses on implementation as a desired outcome of change and program initiation, the relationship of initiation and implementation in change efforts and some tools that can be used to assist implementation efforts. Chapter 4, "Facilitating Coordination and Collaboration of Tasks," emphasizes the people component of implementation. It provides information about the roles that various groups and individuals have in implementation and strategies to ensure quality involvement. Chapter 5, "Monitoring Implementation," provides information on the important, but often neglected, formative evaluation component of implementation. A discussion of why monitoring is needed, what tools are available to help, when to monitor, and who should do it is included. The differences in content and process evaluation and why each is important is also presented. The formative evaluation focus of monitoring implementation is directly related to a discussion on making needed adjustments. Topics treated include: data analyses, uses of data for planning and decision making, and establishing feedback systems to identify needed corrections and reporting to others, and developing the continuous feedback loop. Chapter 6, "Supporting Those Responsible for Implementation," emphasizes the need for on-going support, training, and resources to achieve satisfactory levels of implementation. The admonition for "supporting those responsible" is inclusive, encompassing top management, building leaders, classroom personnel, support staff, and community. Knowledge and skills regarding effective staff development, delegation of responsibility and authority, organizational issues as supports or barriers, and professional growth for self and others form the major elements of the chapter. Finally, the conclusion in Chapter 7, "Closing with a Few Brief Reflections," contains five recommended behaviors. Each of the recommended behaviors requires numerous knowledge and skills. However, while they appear in the closing chapter of the book, they are offered as places to start in pursuing successful implementation. A reference list of the works used in this volume follows Chapter 7.

IMPLEMENTATION: ONE OF TWENTY-ONE

It would be difficult, if not impossible, to discuss implementation without also referencing the other 20 domains both in this introduction and throughout the volume. Implementation calls for a synthesis of knowledge and skills from all other domains. For example, moving from plan to practice can only be accomplished with skilled leadership. Among other things, leadership provides the means to develop the vision, set the direction, and initiate the planning that identifies what needs to be implemented. Also, the identification of need, the monitoring of progress, the feedback from individuals and groups regarding direction and concerns and myriad other important components of implementation cannot be done without knowledge and skills in information collection. Judgment provides yet another example of how knowledge and skills from other domains relate to implementation. Judging, when done well, helps assure that the projects, programs, and so forth that we seek to implement are worthy of the time and effort they demand. Additionally, judgment is crucial in determining such things as which changes to resist and which to embrace, what strategy adjustments to make and when, and what support to provide, when and to whom. Implementation is all of the above and more. It is one of the 21 domains of knowledge and skills principals must master to effectively direct what they and teachers do—implement. What kind of leadership has occurred if there is no effective implementation? Are philosophical and cultural values not evidenced in what we implement and how we do it? Does not motivating others require implementation and are we not attempting to motivate them in an effort to implement something? One or more connections of this sort can be drawn between implementation and each of the other 20 domains. But the perspective here is more than connections. It is the image of the riverbed of "converging streams of behavior" distilled from its companion domains which finds expression in effective implementation.

FOLLOW-UP ACTIVITIES

1. Secure a copy of the NPBEA's "21 Domains of Knowledge and Skills." Read the descriptions of each of the other 20 domains. Using a web or spoke diagram, draw a visual which

represents your responses to the question, "Are knowledge and skills from this domain required for successful implementation?" for each of the other 20 domains. When you have finished your web or spoke, reread the section in Chapter 1 entitled "One of Twenty-one."

2. Select two recent change initiatives in your school or district. Choose one of the initiatives because of its success and the other because of difficulties being experienced in getting it implemented. Use the other 20 domains from NPBEA's to make some initial assessments on the relationship between each of these domains and the levels of success of the two initiatives. Place a brief description of each change initiative at the top of a blank page. Immediately under the description, draw three columns. Label the columns as Domains, + and – . List each of the 20 domains down the left side of the page under the column heading of "Domains." Next, rate each of the domains as a plus or a minus in relationship to the change initiative described at the top of the page.

For each domain, make an assessment regarding its presence in supporting the change initiative. For example, in thinking about the Staff Development Domain in relationship to each of the change initiatives selected (one successfully implemented, one less successfully implemented), rate the level at which participants' professional needs were identified, programs to improve staff effectiveness were planned and organized, individuals and groups were supervised, and so forth, and check either the plus or minus column. Do this for each of the selected change initiatives with each of the other 20 domains. Are more of the 20 domains checked in the + column on the more successfully implemented initiative than on the initiatives experiencing less success?

SAMPLE FORM FOR FOLLOW-UP ACTIVITY #2

Change initiative: Teachers planning and delivering instructional concepts as interdisciplinary teams.

Domains	+	−

I. Functional Domains

Leadership
Information Collection
Problem Analysis
Judgment
Organizational Oversight
Implementation
Delegation

II. Program Domains

Instructional Program
Curriculum Design
Student Guidance and Development
Staff Development
Measurement and Evaluation
Resource Allocation

III. Interpersonal Domains

Motivating Others
Sensitivity
Oral Expression
Written Expression

IV. Contextual Domains

Philosophical and Cultural Values
Legal and Regulatory Applications
Policy and Political Influences
Public and Media Relationships

2

MAKING THINGS HAPPEN

AN OVERVIEW OF WHAT PRINCIPALS HAVE TO MAKE HAPPEN

Principals need to know about implementation. As the title of this chapter suggests, implementation is the point at which things move beyond talking and planning and really begin to happen. However, implementation is not some kind of event associated only with new activities. Principals have to make things happen all of the time. Any principal who isn't successfully implementing all kinds of things everyday, won't be a principal very long!

Think about it! Every day school has to open; students need to arrive safely; teachers need to be at school ready to work with students; teachers and office staff need to work together to report student attendance; the food service personnel need to serve lunch to students and staff; and on and on it goes. Each of these things (and many, many others) must happen every day. Principals must implement them or see that they are implemented. It is important to realize that successful principals already know a great deal about implementation and use it daily. Most people have been successfully implementing all kinds of things since they were kids—games, teamwork, football plays, a camping trip, programming a VCR, getting the desired new outfit, and so forth. Because principals were kids once, most have a long history of being successful implementers. As teachers, principals were also required to be skilled implementers. Implementation was a constant in their classrooms; something was always at some stage of implementation—math lessons, science experiments, classroom management, fund raisers, new programs, innovations, and so on. Successful implementation of classroom activities and processes provided an excellent experience base. Principals must continue to fine tune the skills that have made them successful implementers for so long. How principals go about "making things happen" or "how they go about implementing" is what this chapter is about. Three types of implementation—routine, new or nonroutine, and unique—are identified. Eight conditions or organizational characteristics of successful implementation of routine activities are identified. Additionally, a section on how new programs and practices get started and continue or disappear is summarized with seven common characteristics of successful implementation of new or nonroutine activities. The third type of implementation, unique, is divided into two subgroups—unusual nonemergency and crisis/disasters. Examples of what events this third type of implementation might include and what conditions need to be in place for successful implementation are presented. Throughout the discussion of the implementation types, references are made to the levels of responsibility the principal has for each. The chapter ends with a summary that reinforces the idea that principals already know a great deal about implementation and how important it is to continue developing this knowledge/skill domain.

TYPES OF IMPLEMENTATION AND LEVELS OF RESPONSIBILITY FOR IMPLEMENTING

Implementation (making things happen) can vary in kind or type. Some implementation events are routine, others are new, and some are unique (happening only once or infrequently). While each of these types is different, when successfully done, they have some common characteristics or elements that are worth noting. The same is true when they are not successfully done; the characteristics or elements of failure can also help us, that is, learning from our mistakes. The levels of responsibilities that principals have in implementation efforts vary. Sometimes principals are directly involved in implementation efforts. Sometimes they are directly involved initially but delegate continuation efforts to others. In still other instances, principals may find their level of responsibility to be that of supporting individuals so they can "make things happen." The levels of responsibility that principals have for implementation are to some degree related to the types of implementation. As the different types of implementation are explored, their relationship to levels of responsibility must also be examined.

IMPLEMENTATION TYPE: ROUTINE

Many things are routinely implemented in schools. One way of thinking about routine is that if you're doing a good job, hardly anyone notices; it is just "the way things are." In fact, when someone asks what we do or how we do it, it is often difficult to respond; it is hard to describe just what and how it happens—it just does. Routine can be compared to the notion of "automaticity" in physical functions and learning functions. When we first try certain behaviors/skills, we are awkward; we have to concentrate, give them considerable thought, and make sure every action is done correctly and in the proper sequence. After practicing for a period of time, the behavior becomes automatic; there is no longer much thought needed to make it happen—it becomes almost unconscious. The actions needed to drive a car, to participate in a practiced sport (skiing, swimming, bicycling, etc.), or to translate groups of letters into meaningful words once you've learned to read, are all examples of behaviors that at one time required careful thought, but with practice eventually became automatic and routine.

Beginning principals, or those new to a school, are well-advised to pay particular attention to "routine implementation." Starting the school year can be a particularly stressful time. Opening and closing times, bus schedules, lunch schedules, paying fees, classroom assignments, health records, and proper contact persons to call about problems are examples of "routine implementation" that require careful attention. If well done, the opening day and week of school can be relatively pleasant for all concerned. If not, expect trouble that may linger well into the school year. Likewise, any change in the "routine" at any time of the school year (beginning or during) can trigger a "firestorm" of confusion and hostility if not properly attended to "before the fact." People will be tolerant of emergencies but not of careless oversight. Principals must be skilled implementers of the "routine." Routine is not a bad thing. Without some level of routine in our personal and work lives stress would likely overtake us. Some of life needs to be predictable and automatic. Establishing routines can help us gain time and

energy to focus on other activities. Standard operating procedures can be most helpful in implementing school activities.
Routines create a stability and predictability that assure teachers, students, parents and staff that school will "happen." Some
of the things in schools that tend to become routine are:

- Daily
  - opening school each day
  - getting students to school each day
  - feeding students
  - class and activity schedules
  - making sure everyone has a classroom and ma-
    terials
  - assuring a safe and orderly environment
  - cleaning of the building
  - orderly movement within the building
  - initiation of instruction
  - taking and reporting attendance

Some of the things that are for the most part routine, but occur
only periodically are:

- Routine but periodic:
  - maintenance of building and equipment
  - assigning students to classrooms
  - identifying eligibility for special services place-
    ments
  - hiring personnel
  - student assembly procedures
  - annual starting and closing of the school year
  - creating a master schedule
  - adjusting to a new superintendent

Each of the activities requires that a number of different
things be done by a variety of people in order to be accomplished successfully. Yet, scanning the list confirms that with
few exceptions these things happen daily in schools across the
nation. What are some of the "conditions" or organizational

characteristics that insure the successful implementation of routine activities?

COMMON CHARACTERISTICS OF SUCCESSFUL ROUTINE IMPLEMENTATION

♦ Clear expectations for what is to happen and the procedures for accomplishing it are stated.

There is a kind of SOP (standard operating procedure) aura about these activities. Often what is to happen and how are captured in written form. Handbooks, policy manuals, master contracts, informational meetings, and other means of information dissemination are created to be sure that the expectations for "what" and the procedures for "how " are clear and available at any time.

♦ Time to practice and learn what to do and how to do it is provided.

Routine activities generally happen frequently. This gives everyone plenty of time to learn what to do and how to do it. Not much time lapses between one implementation event and the next, so there is not much time to forget what happened the previous day or hour, which makes the next attempt even easier.

♦ A general understanding of reasons for and acceptance of why successful implementation of this activity is important.

Whether it involves orderly procedures for entering the building to begin the school day or for a tornado alert, everyone has been informed as to why this needs to be methodical and systematic. Written statements about these activities are often prefaced in handbooks, newsletters, and informational meetings with something like, "in order to assure that..."; the why is made clear early on and to everyone.

♦ Everybody helps everybody else get it right.

Those who know help those who need to know learn how. There is a kind of group responsibility for making these things happen. Everybody seems to know what to do, and for anyone who doesn't there is someone willing to teach them. When any member of the organization sees someone not following the routine, some action is taken. This can be done in a number of ways—a simple comment, modeling, formal lessons, or rewards and sanctions.

♦ Monitoring with feedback and opportunities to adjust/correct must be in place.

Someone is always "watching" to be sure these things happen as planned. Things are never allowed to get too far astray from the expected before someone is correcting and bringing actual behavior back into line with the planned behavior.

♦ Those who have a part in the process give input on how things are going and what might make them go even better.

Perhaps because so many people are involved in many of these activities, feedback on how things are going is often sought from a variety of stakeholders. Phone calls of complaint, feedback from supervisors and workers, student and parent surveys, teachers' concerns, and other sources are used and even sought as ways of knowing "how things are going" and "what needs to be changed."

♦ Once a desired level of success is achieved, these activities are not often changed.

These routines become examples of the classic "if it ain't broke don't fix it" adage. The activities achieve the intended outcome(s); for example, children arrive at school on-time and safe; students and staff move about the building without injury or incidents; all classrooms are staffed with a teacher (regular staff or substitutes); and so on. When changes are made in these activities, it is generally after the need to do so has been clearly identified. Even then only those processes and/or procedures absolutely necessary to return to the desired level of performance will be changed.

♦ The needed materials, personnel, and other components are in place and continue to be provided to make this happen.

The necessary supports (human and nonhuman) are allocated regularly. They are automatically included in budgeting procedures and responsibility rosters. There never is a question about whether the resources for these routines should or should not be allocated. In fact, it is more likely that there are contingency plans on what to do to make sure these activities occur even if there is a shortage or disruption in the materials, manpower, or other components needed.

Principals have a variety of responsibility levels in establishing and maintaining the implementation of routine activities. When routines are being established, principals are directly and heavily involved. They work with the planning, with getting feedback from others involved, with making sure procedures and processes are legal, by coordinating with other units of the organization, by disseminating the needed explanation and expectations, and by securing the correct amount and kinds of resources. Once the activities are established as routine they take on a life of their own and "run on automatic." Checking on them occasionally is important in maintaining these activities. Once established, principals can sometimes delegate the maintenance of these activities to others. However, it is important to remember that principals are always responsible for the activities in their building. Any delegation must always be done with care and the understanding that ultimately principals are responsible for whatever happens.

In short, once established, routine activities are implemented with a level of automaticity and do not require constant focused attention. However, when something unfamiliar occurs to disrupt the routine or some important aspect necessary to the operation is missing, conscious efforts must be made to think about how to establish or reestablish the routine. For example, when it is a new school year, many students, parents, and teachers new to the school don't know the routines for arrival, dismissal, lunch, pep rallies, and so forth. This is the time to review the eight characteristics of successful routine implementation and take appropriate action. Principals have many demands on their time and energy. Early in the school year, the amount of time and energy needed to "learn the ropes" will be generously accommodated. However, as the school year gets underway, parents, students, staff, supervisors, and others want more of the principal's time and energy devoted to new initiatives and problem situations. The sooner the principal can get routine implementation in place the sooner time and energy can be reallocated to other types of implementation. Routine implementation is directly responsible for making many things happen. Because routine implementation frees the time, energy, and focus of people in the school, these precious resources become available for other implementation projects.

IMPLEMENTATION TYPE: NEW (NONROUTINE)

This type of implementation focuses on activities or procedures such as new instructional programs, use of new materials, adoption of new teaching methods, and changes in the law/school code. Implementation of these kinds of changes is often described as moving through three sequential stages: initiation, implementation, and continuation/institutionalization. A rich collection of research literature describes implementation as a stage of the change process (Conner, 1993; Fullan, 1991; Harvey, 1990; Hord, Rutherford, Huling-Austin, & Hall, 1987; Pankake, 1996; Pankake & Palmer, 1996; and Quaglia, 1991). Many studies have identified several elements characteristic of successful implementation. Those that follow are based on a variety of sources from the literature in this area.

COMMON CHARACTERISTICS OF SUCCESSFUL NEW IMPLEMENTATION

- ♦ The necessary resources to support the new effort or project are consistently available.

New programs/projects that achieve successful implementation have continued support. Personnel, materials, and other costs become regular budget items.

Projects that are submitted and approved for the next school year generally include resource needs in the form of staffing and operating budgets. Unfortunately, after the first year or two of full resource support, reductions often occur. These might come in the form of fewer people assigned to the project or as significant decreases in the money available to replace materials or to carry out needed staff development. However, the amount of resources required to maintain and sustain a program or project rarely decreases. In fact, as some efforts succeed, additional resources will be needed. Especially if new programs or projects are supported at initiation through external grants, provisions need to be made to incorporate the needed resources for maintaining the program or project into the regular school/district budget. If not, the improvements made during the fully supported initiation phase of the project will disappear along with the support.

Reading Recovery is a program in many schools that can be used as an example of this characteristic. If Reading Recovery is to continue accomplishing the goals for which it was adopted and implemented, it must continue to receive support. Cutting back on numbers and training of staff may appear to cut costs; however, in reality, the results will be that the program will not continue to be implemented at the quantity or quality levels intended. Another example might involve a math improvement project. If the project resources were approved as proposed and later a 20% reduction in costs is demanded, a determination of whether this can be done without seriously damaging the planned program must be made. It may be better to abandon the project than to try to operate on resources inadequate for accomplishing the intended results.

  ♦ Those who are trying to implement view the new
    effort or project as doable or usable.

Fullan (1991) refers to this as the "practicality ethic." If, early on, the implementers do not perceive that the required activities are meaningful and manageable, they will not be continued. Projects, programs and materials that may sound good but do not fit the "reality" of the users do not get implemented.

Principals and others who are informed (knowledgeable) about past and present practice in education under the banner of "needed change" are quite aware of how often failed efforts are due to neglecting those who must do the implementing. State legislators are learning this, as are local school boards and superintendents. People are not very tolerant of "surprises" that impact (great or small) their personal or professional lives. Principals should make every effort to insure that they and their staff are not "surprised"—no matter the source. Additionally, they should not volunteer themselves or others to do the impossible or impractical.

Examples of this characteristic are plentiful. I recall making an effort to encourage the teaching of science with an emphasis on inquiry approaches in all classrooms during my tenure as building principal. To do this, a system needed to be established that insured that each of the science unit resource packages was fully equipped and ready to use. One of the reasons the units were not being used prior to this project was because teachers could never be sure that the packages were complete. When the system began to operate successfully and those using the packages could trust that the materials would be available, more and more instances of teaching science with an emphasis on inquiry approaches occurred; that is, it became doable/usable.

+ Training and continued development of necessary knowledge and skills are ongoing.

New projects/programs are generally initiated with considerable focus on information giving and skill development. There is some evidence to support the notion that training and development are as important during implementation as at any other stage in the change process. New projects and programs that achieve successful implementation devote time, energy and resources to continued training.

Principals must take the lead in determining what new knowledge and skills are needed by those doing the implementing. The "new" here means comparing knowledge/skills required by the program with those possessed by those who must implement it. Thus, needed staff development is defined. Do not overlook students as implementers. What new demands does the program require of them?

Many curricular innovations have faltered or failed because of this oversight. The classic examples of this—the "new math," "open education," and "alphabet science" (ESS, SCIS, BSCS, PSCS, etc.)—are referenced often even after 25 years. Each of these curricular innovations had merit. However, in so many instances, training at a knowledge/theory level was all that was provided to teachers and administrators. Little developmental time was given to the demonstration of how to use these concepts and materials and what strategies were best for teaching and managing them. Rarely were organizational structures changed to allow coaching for teachers as they actually tried these things out with students. The results of this lack of ongoing training and development created some rather vivid memories for many who are still working in schools today. They may be the individuals in your school who are less than enthusiastic about going to professional development sessions on curriculum innovations; you may find them to be among those who question the adoption and initiation of new programs as "a waste of time" or who inform you that, "We did this before and it didn't work then. Why do you think it will now?"; and others may just quietly go on about their daily activities unchanged and convinced that nothing ever really changes.

Technology is another example of assuring that training and continued development of necessary knowledge and skills are ongoing. Getting the equipment installed does not assure its use. Even sending staff to training on the installed equipment will not make it happen. Training and development, in one form or another, must be continuously available at the site where the people and the technology meet and try to work together. Opportunities to practice and get feedback on performance is a must for improving skills. Technology specialists, onsite development labs and other forms of ongoing training and development have been created and used where technology has been successfully implemented.

♦ Progress checks are done on a continuous basis.

This assures that things are proceeding as planned. If it is discovered that they are not, corrections are made immediately.

Are students learning what is expected when it is expected? Are effective instructional adjustments being made? Do teachers appear to have the knowledge/skills they need? Are they using them effectively? Finding the answers to these kinds of questions involves doing progress checks. Progress checks not only need to be done, but they need to be done continuously. For example, an answer to the question, "Are students learning what is expected when it is expected?" can be given in May of each school year. However, if the answer is "no," it is too late to enact any needed changes. Continuous checks would have information about student learning being collected more frequently, perhaps in September, November, and February, as well as May. With each progress check adjustments are possible so that in May a positive response to "Are students learning what is expected when it is expected?" can be asserted and demonstrated! Similarly, asking teachers in May if they had the knowledge and skills they needed to teach the new program is, to say the least, after the fact. Checking progress continuously would require that this question be posed frequently; the responses to the question would be used to plan and implement needed staff development throughout the year.

♦ Feedback based on the progress checks is supplied frequently to those responsible for the implementation.

Progress checks are important, but unless that information is given to the individuals responsible for implementation, quality control benefits are lost. Successful implementation requires communication mechanisms that provide a feedback loop that informs "implementers" regarding progress.

How often does the principal and/or a designee meet with teachers, individually and in groups, where the focus is on program implementation progress? How often are schoolwide data synthesized and reported internally, to central office, and to parents? Providing information for improvement is essential if successful new implementation is to result. Information tells us how things are going; feedback lets us know how things can be made better.

For example, if student achievement data indicate that students are having difficulty with the concepts of ratios and proportions but that information is never shared with classroom teachers and students, no adjustments relative to this will be made; therefore, any resulting improvement in these areas would occur by chance not by design. If, however, the information is fed back to teachers and students, then a variety of adjustments might result. For example, changes might be made in allocated time for teaching, guided practice, and review; changes in the sequencing of teaching units might be made to assure these concepts are taught prior to testing; supplemental teaching materials on these concepts might be purchased; or staff development sessions on effective teaching strategies for these concepts might be established. Information is useful only if it is fed back frequently to those who need it to check their progress and make adjustments to improve.

♦ Somebody or several somebodies are serving as cheerleaders and/or coaches for the project/program's use.

When advocacy for the programs/projects wanes, the programs/projects often do the same. The ones that are successfully implemented are those that have continued advocacy and commitment by large numbers of individuals, including those in key leadership positions.

Principals must be the leaders in this group of cheerleaders. If properly done, relevant others will provide voluntary testimony and assist in the facilitation of the program/project. Teachers and parents will acknowledge it. So will students. (In a real sense, they, too, become cheerleaders.) Some of the early works regarding effective schools speak to the power of this characteristic to support or prevent successful implementation. Benjamin (1981) told a variety of stories about effective schools and the individual principals and teaching staffs working in them. Where the efforts for improvement were adopted by the teachers, parents, and students, as well as the principal, the changes in the schools' programs were successfully implemented. In schools where the innovation was solely dependent on the principal for advocacy, when the principal left, so did the programs/projects and improvement efforts. An example of the same characteristic influencing positively can be seen in Cooper, Texas. In this district, the board, superintendent, elementary principal, and teachers entered into a curriculum development project in the areas of reading, math, science, and social studies. Teachers from the district worked with representatives from Policy Studies in Education to identify learning objectives for the students in Cooper ISD. Even more involvement and advocacy surfaced when teachers began to work within and between grade levels in identifying materials for teaching objectives, determining pacing schedules for teaching objectives, and exchanging strategies for effective instruction. As the school year got underway, the Policy Studies representatives took the work regarding pacing schedules for teaching objectives and converted it into checklists of objectives to be taught by subject, grade level, and semester, for distribution to the parents of students in Cooper ISD. Not long into the school year, teachers in Cooper reported parents were not only openly pleased about knowing what their children were learning, but were even sending in items that they thought could assist teachers in their instruction on these objectives. The story serves to demonstrate how having the enthusiasm of the board and superintendent are important variables. However, the principal's, teachers', and parents' advocacy is what sustains this innovation and supports its full and continued implementation.

♦ Programs/projects that achieve implementation status are those that have clear purposes and direction.

This clarity serves as a compass pointing toward the directions for the next steps implementers should take. The purposes of a program, when clear, provide a template for comparison of where we are in relationship to where we want to be. This makes it easier to set goals and conduct progress checks essential to continued successful implementation.

Vague, wordy, or mystical goal or purpose statements probably do more harm than good. They reflect the meaning embodied in the notion "that if you don't know or don't care where you are going, any route will take you there." For example, improving literacy sounds like a decent goal. However, it doesn't indicate anything about who, when, what kind or how much improvement is sought. Meaningful goal/purpose statements do. Developing goal statements focused on student performance was emphasized at a workshop on goal setting and improvement planning in Turner Community School District, Kansas City, Kansas. The Turner CSD staff has been actively working on a variety of school improvement projects over the last two years and many of the decision-making structures, school climate issues, and staff development efforts have resulted in renewed energy and enthusiasm for the staff and administration. With this renewal foundation in place, it was time to go beyond "improve" statements in order to clearly indicate that all of the activities and projects occurring in the district were to result in measurable differences in student performance.

While this list is not exhaustive, it does provide an overview of characteristics found repeatedly in successful implementation efforts: clear purposes and directions, continued advocacy, resource support, continued training and development, regular progress checks, mechanisms to provide continuous feedback, and the general belief by implementers that the project/program is both useful to do and capable of being done.

IMPLEMENTATION TYPE: UNIQUE

Some things that need to be implemented successfully happen rarely—perhaps only once in a career. These are things such as a visit from the governor or president, construction of a new facility, or consolidation of schools/school districts. These happenings are generally less localized and involve a variety of individuals from all levels of the organization and often several organizations outside education. As a result, principals are likely to be less involved in the planning and directing role and more in the receiver-doer role.

In the case of visiting dignitaries, a principal may be called on to arrange entertainment for the event—choral, or instrumental, or both. Or the school may house a unique facility (radio or television station, for example) and there will be an onsite visit. Security issues are always of concern when high profile guests are in the school. Such assignments should be treated as implementation projects with all the relevant principles and practices being observed. In the cases of new construction and consolidation, involvement will most likely be determined by the project's impact on the principal's school and/or any special expertise the principal possesses.

Still, the same issues that are important to school level routines and new program/project implementations are important here. In this instance, however, the principal will need to secure them rather than create them. For example, clear expectations of what school personnel are to do and procedures for how it is to happen must be requested. Questions regarding who is to provide training and development and how to finance it need to be answered. Additionally, those who will conduct meetings and draft written documents for disseminating information explaining the project/event must be identified.

Securing this information and seeing that the appropriate individuals are informed and understand it are major responsibilities for the principal in this type of implementation. Knowledge and skills in communication, organization, and judgment are basic criteria principals will need for successful implementation of unique events/processes. While responsibility for the successful implementation of the event may fall to someone external to the school (government security officers, architect/general contractor, superintendent and the board) principals will still be responsible for the parts delegated to them and their staffs. Implementing these parts successfully will directly affect the event/project as a whole. So, while the responsibility level for unique implementation may differ in degree, it does not differ in kind from any other implementation type.

Another category of unique activities/procedures that needs to be successfully implemented is that which deals with disasters and/or crises. School disasters/crises include such situations as fires, tornadoes, death of a teacher, student suicide, drive-by shooting, school bus accident, and severe injury of student or staff. While we hope never to have to implement the actions/procedures developed for such situations, when it must be done, complete, appropriate, and efficient implementation must occur. While these are far from routine situations, the characteristics of effective routines can assist in developing and implementing complete, appropriate, and efficient actions for dealing with disasters/crises:

- Expectations and procedures to be followed must be clear.
- Procedures must be taught and practiced regularly.
- Procedures must be monitored and corrections/ adjustments made when necessary.
- Everyone must know about the procedures and understand why they must be followed.
- Resources must be available for implementation at all times.

A principal's responsibility here is grave. Whether these actions are ever used for their intended purpose is not the issue. Principals must be ready and be sure that everyone within their organization is ready and able to successfully implement these processes/procedures.

SUMMARY

A common quote in the change literature indicates that "change is a process and not an event" (Hord et al., 1987). This is also true for implementation. Implementation does not just happen one day. It takes place over time, often with progress occurring in "chunks," sometimes in "slivers," and at other times not at all. Conner (1993) describes change as "…[unfolding] on many different levels simultaneously. Instead of relying on hard and fast rules that can get you into trouble, acknowledge the complexity of change by focusing on the patterns and principles for your direction" (p. 10). Viewing implementation as a process and not an event, and seeing it as an unfolding process to be coached, rather than directed, will increase the likelihood of success. Those things that we have successfully made happen throughout our lives were probably handled this way. An encouraging declaration regarding successful implementation was made by Fullan when he noted that an examination of examples of successful change efforts reveals a key feature to be "organized common sense." This aligns well with this chapter's examination of the characteristics of the implementation activities that are successfully done each day in schools everywhere. Principals already have considerable experience with implementation. The information presented here helps enrich this essential knowledge/skill domain.

FOLLOW-UP ACTIVITIES

1. Use the three implementation types discussed in this chapter (routine, new/nonroutine, and unique) to self-assess the activities in your current work situation. Use a three column form to list the three types of implementation operating in your current situation.

2. Use the three implementation types as a framework for discussing establishing classroom operational procedures with new teachers and or teachers new to your school. Have them develop the Common Characteristics of Successful Routine Implementation as a checklist of questions to use in identifying important actions they need to take in establishing classroom routines.

3. Use the feedback form that follows to get feedback regarding the extent to which any new (nonroutine) implementation efforts contain the "common characteristics of success." On the basis of the information you receive, initiate discussions with your faculty and staff on how each of the characteristics might be strengthened.

NEW PROJECT/PROGRAM IMPLEMENTATION
SUCCESS FEEDBACK FORM

Please let me know your perceptions on these items regarding our efforts to implement _____.

	absolutely			*afraid not*		
1. Have the necessary resources to support the new effort or project consistently been made available?	1	2	3	4	5	6
2. Do you believe this effort/ project is doable?	1	2	3	4	5	6
3. Is it usable?	1	2	3	4	5	6
4. Has training and continued development of necessary knowledge and skills been ongoing?	1	2	3	4	5	6
5. Are progress checks being done on a continuous basis?	1	2	3	4	5	6
6. Have you been given frequent feedback based on the progress checks?	1	2	3	4	5	6
7. Are there people who are serving as cheerleaders and coaches for this project/program?	1	2	3	4	5	6
8. Are the purposes and direction of the project/program clear?	1	2	3	4	5	6

3

PUTTING PROGRAMS AND CHANGE EFFORTS INTO ACTION

Knowing what ought to be changed (what) and identifying the necessary means for achieving the change (how) are basic requirements if successful implementation is to be achieved. This statement describes the situation well:

> Most employees in most organizations are readily able to mouth what in their opinion "ought" to be done; only a few are consistently able with equal facility to express a cogent and responsible course of action.... (Lippitt, Langseth, & Mossop, 1985, pp. 94–95).

While Lippitt et al. write from a business perspective, they couldn't have written a more accurate description of educational organizations. It sometimes seems as if everyone (judges, parents, governors, legislators, talk show hosts, etc.) knows what "ought" to change in education. But, as Lippitt and his colleagues note, ideas about how the "oughts" can be implemented successfully are few.

Implementation is directly connected with the change process. It would be difficult to talk about implementation without also talking about planned change. The literature on change plays a crucial role in developing and presenting the necessary concepts to convey the who, what, when, where, and how of implementation.

Change as a phenomenon has received a great deal of attention lately. Everyone seems to be studying it, writing about it, presenting a workshop on it, or doing all three. At this time, we could probably fill a nice-sized room with what we know about change. Unfortunately, we would also need another room of at least equal size to store all of the unanswered questions and information regarding what we don't know about change and the change process. However, just because we don't know everything doesn't mean we shouldn't use everything we do know. There has been some important work done in this area and the knowledge generated can be helpful to us in becoming skilled implementers.

During the 30-plus years in which planned change has been researched, the implementation successes have been comparatively few. Given the number of initiations offered over that time period, the ratio of starts to successful finishes is discouraging. According to Quaglia (1991), one of the reasons the starts-to-finishes ratio is so lopsided is because, "Implementation...is the most difficult and complex stage of the [change] process."

However, "difficult and complex" are not synonyms for impossible. Certainly implementation can and does occur. In fact, Fullan (1991) points out there are examples of successfully implemented change efforts, and that no matter where in the world they occur, they share some common elements. And, for our purposes, it is important to recall that one of the key features in these success examples was the presence of what Fullan called, "organized common sense."

So, "difficult and complex" deserve note and due respect; however, they do not deserve a status that cripples our efforts. Certainly it is a big mistake for anyone to assume that proposed changes will be successfully implemented. If effective implementation is to occur, it must be tended to, and that is one of the principal's responsibilities. Additionally, the principal must understand how initiation and implementation are connected. Specifically there is a need to know how initiation influences the success of implementation. Knowing about and using this information will allow principals to take advantage of this initiation-implementation connection in selecting and designing implementation strategies.

This chapter is about "Putting Program and Change Efforts Into Action." Changes and program initiations are just good intentions until they are effectively implemented. The first section deals with the prerequisites for reaching successful implementation: a clear vision, an accurate assessment of the current situation in relationship to the vision, and a willingness to commit to the long-term. The next section, "The Relationship of Initiation and Implementation in Change Efforts," looks at implementation as it is more commonly viewed—a phase of the change process. While this view is more limited, it does allow an exploration, in a readiness context, of such elements as a history of successful implementation efforts, who is involved, and how levels and sources of support influence implementation generally. Finally, the last section, "Tools to Assist Implementation Efforts," returns the focus to the "how" (strategies) of implementation. Activities (tools) that principals can use to help them determine both the need for and ways to implement changes are identified and described.

PREREQUISITES FOR SUCCESSFUL IMPLEMENTATION

THE VISION: WHERE ARE WE GOING?

Unlike a popular athletic shoe advertisement, implementation requires more than "just do it." It is much easier to determine what strategies are required for making something happen if you know for sure just what it is you are trying to accomplish. A prerequisite for successful implementation is a clear description of what will be different when implementation has been achieved. Implementation may be more dependent on this prerequisite than any other element of the change process. This clarity regarding the desired outcome of change travels under several labels. Preparing mission statements, having a vision, and developing purposes or goals are common examples. Fullan (1990) called it "shared meaning" and the Southwest Educational Development Lab (1994) calls it developing an "implementation configuration."

Whatever the terminology, an important aspect of "making it happen" is to see and help others see exactly what "it" is. Being able to describe to others the desired outcome or vision with clarity is essential in helping people implement successfully.

This clear vision or defined purpose is what Shelly (1995) called "the magnet to draw folks through the process." Covey, in his 1989 work *The 7 Habits of Highly Effective People*, admonished that we need to "begin with the end in mind." While

Covey's words were particularly intended to assist with personal change, they are also relevant to the implementation of changes in other areas of life as well; for example, programs, projects, practices. According to Covey (1989), "To begin with the end in mind means to start with a clear understanding of your destination. It means to know where you're going so that you better understand where you are now and so that the steps you take are always in the right direction" (p. 98).

Similarly, over 20 years ago Lakein (1973) pointed out that "control begins with planning. Planning is bringing the future into the present so that you can do something about it now" (p. 25). Answering the question, "Where is it you want to go?," is another way of getting at a definition of the vision. Generating a response to this question results in the setting of goals and objectives, which in turn allow the assessment of where you are in relationship to where you want to be to begin (Pankake, 1986–87).

A part of visioning is to help define the future state and the benefits associated with it. Being able to "see" where we are headed, "why" we need to go there, and what things will look like and be like when we "arrive," helps individuals overcome some of their fears of the unknown and become more active in "making things happen." Principals must spend time *thinking* about and formulating a clear vision for the school. When someone asks, "Why are we changing?" or "How is this going to be any different from what we've been doing?" (and they will), the response needs to be a rich, detailed, comprehensive description of the desired outcomes.

Consider the example of an elementary school math program. The math program in the school is not meeting district expectations regarding student achievement. A careful analysis of student learning data reveals that some students are doing very well in math, others are doing fairly well, and some are having serious problems. It appears that the onset of the problem occurs in the early primary grades K-2. Additionally, the lower achieving students do not seem to make up this loss in subsequent years. Armed with this information, the principal can target change efforts by building on existing strengths while isolating those areas needing special attention. The what and why questions can be addressed meaningfully, keeping hostility and resistance to a minimum.

Once the "end" is clear, the second prerequisite for successful implementation can proceed. The second prerequisite calls for a comprehensive description of the school's current status in relationship to the implementation project's goals and objectives, the means for achieving them, the needed methods and materials for evaluating progress, and the expected or desired results.

ASSESSING THE CURRENT STATUS: WHERE ARE WE NOW?

Principals who expect to achieve successful implementation will need to have knowledge and skills that help them determine their current situation or status.

Knowing the current situation or status is essential in helping with such components as selecting the appropriate activities to pursue, allocating resources to support the selected activities, establishing time lines for completion, collecting informative data, and establishing criteria for determining progress.

The discrepancy between the current status and the vision or desired goal defines the playing field for implementation. Knowing the discrepancy between the two is so important. It will help us to:

♦ Know how to proceed.

If you have ever been lost, the importance of knowing where you are in knowing how to proceed needs little explanation or justification. For anyone who has missed such an experience, imagine being in a dark room with your desired destination a door that leads outside to the sunlight. As you try to determine your "next steps," it would be helpful to know whether the door is behind you, in front of you, to your left, or to your right. It would be helpful to know if you are only a few steps away or quite some distance. If you knew where in the room you were standing and what direction you were currently facing, you could more easily determine which direction to move to reach the door. Without such information, you will grope, stumble, and hope you are heading the right way. The same is true for programs, projects, and processes in schools. Knowing the current situation or status positively facilitates implementation efforts.

♦ Know the kinds and amounts of resources needed to accomplish the journey or reach the goal.

Implementation of any program, project, or process requires resources. Accurate estimates of both the kinds and amounts of resources needed help with several aspects of implementation, including planning, securing long-term commitment and support from others, reducing resistance to change and facilitating the coordination of tasks. Having too much of one thing and not enough of another, and having waste and wants cannot be avoided completely, but they can be minimized if an inventory of needed resources is known.

♦ Develop baseline data and comparison standards for monitoring progress.

Developing baseline data and comparison standards are requirements for monitoring progress and establishing criteria for making midcourse corrections. It's like setting the odometer at zero before you start the trip, or drawing a line in the dirt for the beginning of the race, or making the mark on the door facing at your child's height at age two, or hundreds of other actions we take in our personal and professional lives to mark where we started something. Knowing where we started helps us to measure how we have progressed. Without a measure of where we started, we can only guess at how far we may have come, how far and fast the race was run, or how tall we have really grown.

The same is true with projects, processes, or programs we want to successfully implement in schools. Without a rich description of the current situation it will be impossible to know if we are better, or doing more, or if something is happening more often, or if everyone is happier or more satisfied, or if something takes less time than it did before. If these comparisons are to be made, then there must be baseline information developed for future reference. Time spent developing descriptions of the current situation will prove its worth as things get under way and the question becomes, "Are we making progress?"

♦ Help everyone (even those who can't or won't see the vision) gain a sense of need for change.

If individuals see a need for change they are more likely to embrace it. Initiators view their proposed changes as needed, but others may not; and, they won't take action to make things happen until they do see the need (Pankake, 1996). Harvey

(1990) suggested that initiators develop a written response to the question, "What facts show the need for this change?" (p. 55). Creating a rich description of the current situation or status is a way of responding to Harvey's question. Gathering a variety of information about what is currently happening can be eye-opening. Information well presented can cause us to question our assumptions and examine our perception of how we think things are. Results of surveys, disaggregation of information by subgroupings, examination of graduation rates, a comparison of academic performance records of retained versus not retained students, and hundreds of other information sets can be eye-opening for many people.

♦ Provide an opportunity to practice some skills and applications of knowledge in preparation for the work ahead.

Describing the current situation requires decisions about what information should be included to make the description complete and rich. Skills in data gathering, reporting, interpretation, and decision-making will be utilized. These same skills will be used repeatedly as implementation proceeds. Important questions, opportunities for trial and error, discovery of what data are available and in what form, discovery of data that need to be generated, decisions about tools to use, and experiments on the best ways to present information can all be addressed in these early stages when commitment and enthusiasm for the project are at their highest.

♦ See the "big picture" and identify which parts need attention.

Seeing the "big picture" can be facilitated through the process of creating a rich description of the current situation. Collecting, displaying, and reporting the information needed to describe the current situation allows the viewing of all of the parts of a situation as they fit together to form the whole. Seeing a situation in its entirety enables the interrelationships of the individual parts to be understood. Failure to grasp the "big picture" allows the proposed program or project to be perceived as isolated or independent, thus jeopardizing successful implementation. When creating a description of the current situation, compare the "constellation of support" needed for successful implementation as described in the project plan with what exists now. This activity will assist project personnel to appreciate the "systems" nature of school improvement work.

 ◆ Provide a framework within which to coordinate tasks.

Once the description of the current situation exists, a framework of who, what, when, where, how, and at what quality level things are to function can be established. Within this framework some starting points for identification of tasks, focus areas, information sources, resource needs, personnel development, and responsibility assignments can be sketched. As full-project plans are developed, this framework will be an invaluable guide.

These seven reasons to spend time describing the current situation regarding project implementation illustrate the multiple benefits of such an activity. Without a rich description of the current situation or status, monitoring progress is impossible. It is important to know where you are in relationship to your desired goal or vision if you intend to be able to determine how far you've come as the journey proceeds!

COMMITMENT TO THE LONG-TERM: IS THIS REALLY WHAT WE WANT TO DO?

The third prerequisite for successful implementation is a willingness to commit to a long-term process. Quaglia's (1991) warnings about the difficulty and complexity of change have their roots in the often neglected time lines necessary to achieve real change. In addition to a clear picture of the vision or desired goal, some realistic estimate of just how long it will take to achieve the desired outcome is needed. This long-term time commitment needs to be fully understood from the beginning. Most substantive changes will require three to five years to achieve, and some will take even longer.

The elementary school math program described earlier can also be used to illustrate this point. In the description, reference is made to the onset of the problem occurring in the early primary grades K-2, and the concern that lower achieving students do not make up the loss in subsequent years. To determine if the changes initiated in the K-2 program will result in needed improvements in student learning, a minimum of three years will be needed as the kindergartners involved in the first year of the change efforts move through to grade 2. During this same time period, any changes initiated in grades 3 and above that were intended to help lower achieving students make up losses from the earlier experiences will also need two to three years to evidence themselves as effective or not. Additionally, if a knowledge of whether students can maintain the growth resulting from the changes in K-2 as they move through the improved programming in the upper grades, yet another three to five years of monitoring the student performance will be required. In this example, an implementation period of five or six years will be needed to really determine if the kindergarten students from the program initiation year move on to be high achieving math students in the intermediate or middle school.

Understanding this time element is crucial to everyone involved if implementation is to be successful. "Everyone" in this case refers to community, district level personnel (both policymakers and administrators), teachers, parents, staff, and, perhaps most importantly, the principal. The continued advocacy and long-term commitment of the building principal are key to the successful implementation of any change. Therefore, it is important that the principal understands this and be willing to commit to a long-term process. If the leader of the effort does not understand this or is not willing to make this commitment, it will be impossible to convince others that they should.

Having a clear vision or desired goal (knowing where you want to go), having an accurate assessment of the current situation (knowing where you are now), and having a commitment to the long-term process (knowing that this is what you really want to do) are prerequisites to successful implementation. Failure to adequately satisfy any one of these three demands will almost certainly result in yet another example of a lost opportunity to improve our schools.

THE RELATIONSHIP BETWEEN INITIATION AND IMPLEMENTATION IN CHANGE EFFORTS

Initiation is the first of three general phases of the change process. At the initiation phase, the program change is introduced and a decision is made to pursue it. At the implementation phase, action is taken to put the new program or practice in place. And, finally, it is at the continuation or institutionalization phase that a decision (formal or informal) is made about keeping or abandoning the program (Fullan, 1991). In this sequence, initiation precedes implementation. If it hasn't been initiated, it can't be implemented. However, the manner in which plans, projects, innovations, and other changes are initiated can strongly influence the quality of the implementation that does occur.

This relationship between initiation and implementation is important for principals to know about and understand if successful implementation of change is expected. Consider the often heard (and frequently ignored) admonition to "plan the work and work the plan." Initiation can be thought of as "planning the work," not sketching the work. It is not painting it in broad brush strokes, nor preparing a mission statement, nor writing a philosophy, nor listing a series of lofty goals to be realized in some future millennium. All of these activities are legitimate, but do not satisfy the requirements of initiation or planning the work. No matter the nature of the implementation project, failure to tend to initiation will scuttle implementation.

ELEMENTS OF INITIATION: CREATING A CONTEXT FOR IMPLEMENTATION

Creating a context of readiness for implementation is what initiation is all about. This readiness context requires that a variety of elements be in place if successful implementation is to follow. Many of the elements needed for creating a context of readiness at the initiation phase are common to all change efforts. It may be helpful to use a situation to illustrate these points.

Imagine that the school district that employs you as principal (elementary, middle, or senior high school) charges you with developing and then implementing a "world-class" curriculum in reading/language arts, math, and science. You are in the Initiation Phase of this project's development. Consider the following seven elements of initiation in the context of the charge you have been given. Their relevance should be readily apparent.

- ♦ Planning must be done by both initiators and implementers

Effective planning at the initiation phase is important for successful implementation. Sandy (1991) identified the most important partnership in organizations as the one "between the planner and those who must make the plan work." According to him, "the best way to gear your plan for easy conversion to implementation is to organize the logic of the plan in a way that fits the work to be done" (p. 31). This means that the planners and the implementers need to communicate frequently. This will also help with another important readiness element—ownership of the change.

As regards the "world-class curriculum development" situation posed earlier, consider involving a variety of others with differing perspectives in the development process. Certainly, you would want to have representatives of each subject area involved from the very beginning. Additionally, participation by classroom teachers who will be responsible for teaching the curriculum once it is developed will be critical for successful initiation and implementation. Individuals who have staff development responsibilities and others who will be directly involved in securing resources for the project should also be informed and involved at these early stages. Representatives from the district office, especially those whose advocacy for adoption will be necessary, should be kept informed and asked for input as the project develops. Representatives of the school's parents will also benefit from early involvement and their involvement will prove beneficial as implementation gets underway.

♦ Broad-based ownership of the change is needed.

Who gets to be involved in initiating a change influences many factors in implementation. Quaglia (1991) asserts that a change needs ownership, and therefore everyone needs to be involved in the process. Involving those who must implement the change in decision making during the initiation phase can positively influence the chances for successful implementation. Harvey (1990) calls these implementers the "changees." Because implementation will actually require that the "changees" do some things differently, time spent on gaining their input and focusing on their perspectives is essential.

Doing this at the start and continuing the practice over time allows individuals to become "owners." Assuring that both initiators and implementers are included in the planning helps in addressing this element of the context for implementation also. All of the individuals and groups noted previously will be required to make some changes in their behavior if successful implementation is to occur. The sooner these individuals become involved in the planning, the sooner the change will become theirs rather than something imposed on them—this is ownership. Additionally, as you develop and implement a "world-class curriculum" you should consider involving the most immediate consumers of this project, the students themselves. Particularly at the upper elementary grades and through high school, students can provide some important perspectives regarding changes in schools. As receivers of the curriculum being developed, students need ownership in the project because they will be among the front-line "changees."

◆ The need for the change must be established.

Another important element in creating a context of readiness for change is to be sure that the proposed change is needed. People must believe there is a need for the change. Otherwise, only lip service will be given to the change effort and the contrived environment will not support successful implementation. Principals must help create an understanding of the need that encourages the implementers to want to change. They must have evidence that the change is necessary, and this evidence must be disseminated widely. Unless this need is understood and accepted at the initiation phase, support for the change will be short-lived or even nonexistent.

Given that the "world-class curriculum" assignment came as a charge from the district office, some evidence of the need for this change might be assumed. The principal receiving the charge needs to ask some questions and start gathering information to better understand the origins of the charge. Someone determined this change was needed. It is important to establish: what indicators were used in determining the need; what data have been collected to demonstrate the need for this change; what definition of "world-class" is being used; and what indicators will be needed to determine when "world-class" status has been achieved. Additionally, data will need to be collected at the building and classroom levels in order to respond to these same questions and to build a base upon which to begin developing improvement plans. Dissemination of these data should be done frequently and to a variety of groups, both internal and external to the school. The same information that was gathered to support the need for the change will also be helpful in monitoring progress as implementation gets underway.

 ♦ Long-term support must be secured.

Long-term support needs to be secured in the initiation phase as a precondition to continuing the change process. Support comes in a number of forms, including time, personnel commitment, financial resources, materials/equipment, and appropriate training programs for all those involved. An unfortunate but common occurrence with implementation of programs is the reduction of needed support once the effort is underway. Failure to maintain comprehensive support is almost certain to derail the program.

In the example of the principal charged with developing the "world-class curriculum," the development of a three- to five-year plan complete with estimated resource needs should be submitted to the district for approval. Involving the various groups mentioned earlier provides a comprehensive perspective on needed resources. Additionally, broad-based involvement will help foster ownership of the project. The plan itself represents the school's public declaration of intent to pursue this project over an extended time period, that is, three to five years. Similarly, the acceptance of the plan by district officials (board of education and administration) represents the district's public declaration to support the plan over the time period defined. These two acts blend well to make it more likely that the time commitment and resources needed will be secure for the life of the project. Unless this commitment is present at the initiation phase, confidence that successful implementation can proceed will be severely eroded.

 ♦ Advocacy must be gained and maintained at all levels.

Advocacy to get an innovation adopted is obvious; it is the continued advocacy that is often hard to come by and difficult to maintain. The literature is quite clear that successfully implemented changes had initial support and continued to receive support from the top management of the organization. Advocacy at this level is important in garnering resources and coordinating activities at the organizational level. For the district, that means the board of education, superintendent, and central office staff. At the individual school level that means principal, assistant principals, and lead teachers.

It is also essential that the "implementers" be advocates of the proposed change. Providing opportunity for interaction between and among the people "in the trenches" will assist in developing the context of readiness at the initiation phase. Peers serve as a critical source of advocacy for most of us in every phase of our lives. Whether it's which car to purchase, where to go on vacation, which physician or dentist to choose for the family, or almost anything else, the opinion of a peer will heavily influence our thinking. The same thing is true for innovations in schools.

Principals like to hear what other principals think about an issue or program and teachers like to hear other teachers' opinions in helping them formulate their own. The power of peer advocacy in influencing opinions should also be considered when working with students and parents at the initiation phase of change.

♦ Advocacy must not be overdone.

The intensity of advocacy at initiation will influence whether or not a proposed change gets successfully implemented. There is a balance that advocates must maintain that is enthusiastic and persistent but does not become zealous and overbearing.

When the intensity is too great, people will be resistant to the change and unwilling to pursue it. When too low, people will not be positively motivated. In either case, implementation is unlikely.

Meeting the charge of creating a "world-class curriculum" is important. However, as principal it must not become so all consuming that you are perceived as neglecting other important issues. Everyone gets tired of a "one issue" individual. On the one hand, you want to be dedicated to your mission and persistent in your work to accomplish your charge, but you don't want people to get so tired of hearing you address only one issue that they don't want to hear any more about it from you or anyone else! Let individuals voice their concerns and suggestions about all aspects of the operation of the school. Some of this input will relate to the curriculum project; some of it will not. Listening to all concerns and suggestions and hearing the kinds of issues which are important to those responsible for the implementation is not only being sensitive to others, it is being smart. As Covey (1989) noted, seek first to understand before being understood. By knowing the concerns of your staff you will be in a better position to meet their needs. When their needs have been met, they will be in a better position to pursue implementation of the project.

♦ Success breeds success in change efforts.

If the school or district has a history of successful changes the most recent proposals are more likely to succeed. An organization having a reputation for starting but never implementing changes requires different strategies from one with a history of successful implementation. Implementation is unlikely to occur unless an atmosphere of trust and confidence exist. Building trust and confidence take time. Principals must assess this success history in deciding what strategies should be taken.

In our situation as the principal with the charge to create a "world-class curriculum," a little checking to determine the status of any projects that were initiated in the last three to five years would be time well spent. If the last three to five years were riddled with lots of project starts but few successful implementations, caution is warranted. This situation has likely produced some distrust and skepticism of change projects. Moving slowly and in directions that are most likely to experience early success will be the best strategy. On the other hand, if the history of the school indicates that changes in the past have been successful, then moving too slowly could be a negative. In this situation you would be better advised to build on the history of success and move more rapidly and allow a greater degree of risk-taking to occur. Time spent on these elements of initiation is time well spent.

Each of these elements represents a positive strategy in leading change efforts at any level of the organization. Taken together, they provide a system of support that creates a context for implementation to succeed. Because initiation is the essential prerequisite to implementation, taking time to do this phase correctly is critically important to successful implementation.

TOOLS TO ASSIST IMPLEMENTATION EFFORTS

Efforts to implement changes are enhanced when appropriate "tools" is matched to the work to be done. A representative sample of such tools are described in this section. Other tools can be found or created. Principals are encouraged to use them to identify what needs changing, as well as, how best to do it.

FORCE-FIELD ANALYSIS

Kurt Lewin proposed a tool to assist in planning and implementing changes. It is commonly referred to as force-field analysis. Lewin's premise was that there are three stages to the change process—unfreezing the status quo, changing, and then refreezing. He noted that organizations are held in a state of equilibrium by competing forces. When a change is desired and/or needed, these competing forces need to be identified. Some of the forces, according to Lewin, will be driving forces for the change. Others will be forces working to restrain the change. Describing the desired outcome and identifying the restraining and driving forces are essential in determining strategies for pursuing the unfreezing process.

Once the desired outcome is described, two approaches can be taken to begin the unfreezing. First, strategies can be developed to increase the number of driving forces and/or the intensity of the driving forces currently in existence. A second approach is to develop strategies to reduce or eliminate the resisting forces. When driving forces are increased or created and resisting forces are reduced or eliminated, the unfreezing process occurs and the organization begins to change. Change takes place when an imbalance occurs between the sum of restraining forces and the sum of driving forces.

Force-field analysis charts have been developed and used in quality control and/or leadership training in recent years. A variety of forms have been developed to assist groups and individuals in the identification of the two competing forces in their present organizations. One form is presented here (Figure 3.1) and other variations of this tool can be found in Harvey (1990) and Hanson (1991).

An example of just how the form might be used may also be helpful. If a school is planning to change the class assignment of students from single to multiage groupings, the force-field

FIGURE 3.1. A FORCE-FIELD ANALYSIS WORKSHEET EXAMPLE

Description of the Desired Change: students will be assigned to classrooms based on age and achievement criteria that result in heterogeneous groupings for grades kindergarten through third and/or ages 5–8/9.

Driving Forces	Restraining Forces
(Forces Supporting the Desired Change)	(Forces Working Against the Desired Change)
Majority of the primary teachers	Ellen and Marjorie—two highly respected primary teachers are showing resistance to the idea of multiage grouping
A core parent group is advocating the change	
Other schools in our area have initiated the practice	Our current student performance as measured by the state testing program is good
Decreased enrollments over the last two years have freed up classroom spaces	
Our current student performance as measured by the state testing program is good	While we have space available, some renovation will be necessary, but no funds are available this year
Curriculum director in central office is encouraging schools to experiment with grouping practices	Only two staff members have had any training or experience in working with multiage grouping

Intensity Code:

minimal restraint – , moderate restraint = , strong restraint = =
minimal driver +, moderate driver ++, strong driver +++

Strategies to: Increase Drivers

1. Increase parent advocacy group size through visits to schools already using the practice. Also, hold open forums for expression of concerns and obtaining information.

2. Have the curriculum director help set up the staff development sessions and parent group information meetings

Decrease Restrainers

1. Reduce current student performance as a restraint by setting up a reporting system (including schedule for reports) to parents throughout the year so that performance changes can be identified and corrections made immediately

2. Establish staff development sessions to increase knowledge and skill in multiage grouping

3. Send staff members to visit schools already doing multiage grouping

analysis form could be used to assist in identifying both the resisting and driving forces for such a change in practice.

- First, this school might complete the "Description of the Desired Change": with something similar to "students will be assigned to classrooms based on age and achievement criteria that result in heterogeneous groupings for grades kindergarten through third and/or ages 5–8/9."

- Next, time needs to be spent identifying what people, conditions, circumstances, resources, and so forth exist that act to support the desired change of student assignments to classrooms. Likewise, identification of which people, conditions, circumstances, resources, and so forth exist that will work against the initiation and implementation of this change in the way students are assigned to classrooms needs to be made.

- Finally, the individual or group completing the form should brainstorm some strategies for increasing the driving forces and/or decreasing the restraining forces. The most powerful actions employ strategies for both sides of the force-field simultaneously.

Notice in Figure 3.1 that "Our current student performance as measured by the state testing program is good" appears as both a driving and a restraining force. Good performance may be viewed as a strong foundation upon which to build new practices; however, it may also be used as source of resistance from an "if it ain't broke, don't fix it" perspective. Also, specificity varies from specific names (when known) to more global terms such as "a core parent group." This form will help you think through the various possibilities of support and resistance. Getting the ideas on the page is the most important task. Details can be added later.

The same attitude should be used when generating strategies for increasing and decreasing the forces. Decisions about the value or workablility of the strategy is less important at this point than is getting the ideas down on paper.

Rating of the intensity of the forces requires determining the relative power of each force. This rating can be completed prior to generating the strategies for reduction and increase and then again after some possible strategies have been identified. This second rating of intensity helps the individual or group work through the power that any one action may have on the situation.

CHANGE POTENTIAL ANALYSIS CHART

Erlandson (1980) developed a tool to be used in analyzing how various individuals and groups in the school view a proposed change. The tool is called a Change Potential Analysis Chart. Principals can use this tool (a) to determine if a proposed change should be pursued and (b) if so, what strategies might be employed to implement it. Erlandson notes that "this instrument serves to arrange the administrator's knowledge about how various groups in the school organization and its environment perceive and relate to a proposed change" (p. 2).

The Change Potential Analysis Chart helps principals and other building leaders think through who (individual and group) will be involved in and affected by any proposed change. These individuals and groups are listed down the left side of the chart. Once the individuals and groups have been identified, several categories of information about each of them is indicated across the top of the chart.

Once the chart is completed, the principal has an excellent array of data upon which to base strategy selection. As issues are analyzed, the information on the chart can be refined. While the categories are more specific, the purpose of the Change Potential Analysis Chart is similar to that of the Force-Field Analysis Form. A more detailed explanation of the Change Potential Analysis Chart and examples of it may be found in Erlandson's (1997) volume *Organizational Oversight: Planning and Scheduling for Effectiveness*.

BUSINESS PROCESS MAPPING

Business Process Mapping (BPM) is an especially useful tool in discovering points in a process that may be redundant, unnecessary, bottlenecking the flow, and so forth. Another value of this tool is the insight that is gained about what the process involves. Mapping a process is done by creating a flowchart. The flowchart provides a "picture" of the process, as it exists, which can be analyzed to determine where changes are needed; for example, points in the process that can be eliminated, areas that need better coordination, lines of communication that need improvement, redundancies that need to be eliminated, and needed adjustments in resource allocations (Texas Instruments, 1992).

Tools to assist in using BPM are available. Some are simple templates to use with pencil and paper and others with computers. These tools provide consistency regarding the symbols used in the mapping process, such as, diamonds equal "decision points," parallelograms contain "input or output" information, a rectangle represents a "step or activity," and a trapezoid means to "wait." Additionally, arrows are used to indicate direction, circles mean "storage," and a capsule shape indicates that a process/subprocess is involved. Using the symbols from the Basic Process Flowchart Symbols, an example of mapping a process commonly found in schools has been developed (Figure 3.2). The process selected for the example deals with taking a class field trip.

Step One. The first step in flowcharting is to identify the major tasks involved in the process. For the field trip example, major tasks might include:

- ♦ determining destination and date to visit
- ♦ arrange for transportation and scheduling adjustments

Step Two. Next, all of the major subtasks of each larger task must be identified.

For our example, the following subtasks have been identified in the first major task:

- ♦ determining destination and date to visit
  - identify curriculum objectives/unit
  - identify locations related to curriculum objectives/unit
  - call location officials for possible visit dates
  - check school calendar for scheduling conflicts
  - complete and submit "Field Trip Request Form"
  - wait for form's return

FIGURE 3.2. EXAMPLE OF A BPM FLOWCHART

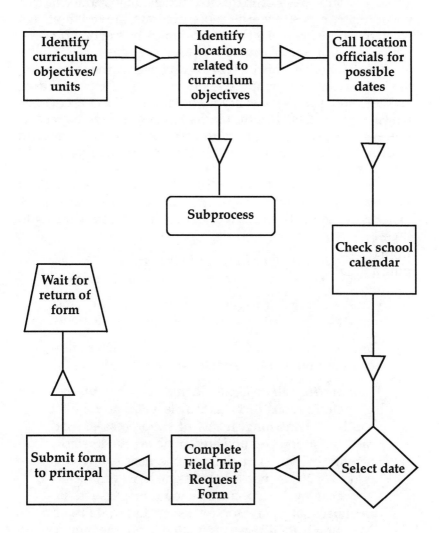

(This process would continue through each of the major tasks. Tasks and subtasks not identified earlier may surface at this step, which is positive. The more accurate the detail at this level, the more likely the chart will depict the existing process, which is important in assessing needed changes.)

Step Three. The third activity is to construct the chart using the basic symbols to map the sequence and influence of each task and subtask. When everyone agrees that the chart depicts the current process, then the discussion and review for needed process changes can begin. With BPM, proposed changes can be done as a "dry run" on paper before any formal proposals or actions are taken.

The TI Manual (1992) identified four "Common Pitfall of Process Flow Charting." While the four were generated from experiences in the business world, they have a familiar ring to them.

Picking too big a process to flow chart. The Process needs to be within the responsibility of the team.

Flow charting at too general a level. The flow chart needs to show all tasks in the process.

Failure to flow chart the process as it is. Don't flow chart as you would like it to be.

Flow charting all tasks at once for a complex process. It's better to construct charts by levels. Start with the top level, consisting mostly of subprocesses. Next, take one subprocess and break it down into its steps / activities. Then start charting the next subprocess, and so on. (Care needs to be taken, however, regarding what level of specificity should be pursued. Remember that the reason for using Business Process Mapping is to increase productivity, not the number of flowcharts!)

Knowing when to use BPM and at what level of detail requires the exercise of judgment by the principal. Principals may stumble into each of the pitfalls before gaining a sense of when and why BPM should be used.

BENCHMARKING

Many things can be benchmarked—strategies, products, services, processes, practices. According to David T. Kearns, the CEO of Xerox Corp. (cited in Camp, 1989), benchmarking is "the continuous process of measuring products, services, and practices against the toughest competitors or those companies recognized as industry leaders" (p. 10). Educators have been engaged in an informal process of benchmarking most of their careers. Teachers adopt methods and materials used by other teachers when these are more effective. Principals are constantly on the lookout for outstanding performance in their own schools. Additionally, they look for "the best" programming and practices in others' schools and districts to learn how to improve their own programs. This searching out and modeling the "best" programs and practices is what benchmarking is all about.

Benchmarking can be done internally or externally. Internally, the "best" practices, functions, services, and products inside the organization are identified and then adopted in other parts of the organization. For example, in a school, a department or program may have trouble getting the paperwork for ordering materials completed correctly and filed on time. This performance, that is, late orders with incorrect paperwork, indicates a need for change. In using benchmarking, the department/program within the school that consistently submits material orders on time and with the correct paperwork would be identified; that is, a model would be located. The department/program having trouble with these processes would investigate how things are done in the model department/unit. The department needing to improve identifies processes from the model department that it can adopt to improve its performance in these activities.

External benchmarking requires that the search for "the best" be made outside the organization. External benchmarking for schools consists of identifying outstanding programs and practices at other schools and then implementing them to improve performance in their own school. Recently, Bruce Wood, superintendent (now retired) of Terrell ISD, Terrell, Texas, led his district in external benchmarking. Dr. Wood told of the district's need to find ways to improve student performance on the high-stakes testing in Texas which is known as

TAAS (Texas Assessment of Academic Skills). In determining improvement strategies, representatives from Terrell ISD visited another school district (Mission ISD). Mission ISD had been identified as a school district that consistently had high student performance on the TAAS Tests. Terrell ISD staff discovered several strategies used by the administrators and teachers in Mission ISD that could be incorporated into or replace processes used in Terrell. After one year of implementing Mission ISD's "best practices" in Terrell, improvement in student performance on the TAAS was tremendous. As this news of Terrell ISD's performance improvement circulated, Terrell became the model for other districts to benchmark. Area school districts are visiting with Terrell staff about the "best practices" they use in improving student performance on the TAAS.

Sometimes external benchmarking is done on organizations not even in the same business but "the best of the best" in a particular service or practice. While schools are institutions of learning, myriad other operations must work well for this mission to be achieved. For example, paperwork has to be processed, food served, internal flow of traffic managed, buildings and grounds maintained and money for various services collected. Looking to other schools for exemplary practices to model is one form of external benchmarking of these processes. However, external benchmarking might also involve looking at organizations other than schools for "best practices" to adopt. Airports might be a good source to look for "best practices" on internal traffic flow. Or a local hotel might have some "best practices" that the school could adopt in feeding large groups of people in very short time periods.

Shiba, Graham, and Walden (1993) identified a number of uses for benchmarking: as a goal-setting mechanism; as a way of planning strategies for improvement; as a way to identify what is important to internal and external publics; as a way to disseminate success stories; and as a way to be proactive in improvement efforts. There are three general categories of activities in the benchmarking process:

- preparation
- data collection and analysis
- using what you learn to improve

Each of these can be subdivided into a variety of steps and/or phases. Individual corporations and organizations have developed unique versions of the benchmarking process. For example, IBM uses four phases: (1) Organize and Plan, (2) Collect Data, (3) Analyze, and (4) Action (Archer, 1994); Xerox's process has five phases (1) Planning, (2) Analysis, (3) Integration, (4) Action, and (5) Return, that is, begin a new benchmarking process (Camp, 1989); and the Center for Excellence (Texas A & M University–Commerce) developed a flowchart to depict steps of the benchmarking process (Pryor, Pankake, & Hoskison, 1995). An essential step in benchmarking is to know what currently exists in your own organization before data are collected from others.

Business Process Mapping can help with the "self-discovery" process of benchmarking. Knowing the details of the current processes in your own organization helps identify those "gaps" between what you do and what "the best of the best" do. Thus, BPM is a tool that can be helpful in using another tool. Having BPM in place helps with the productive use of benchmarking. Following are some of the ways in which benchmarking can help an organization (Pryor, Pankake, & Hoskison, 1995). While the original sources for these were businesses, the benefits are easily translated to schools:

♦ Helps to focus on both the desired results and the methods for achieving them
♦ Provides a means for learning from others
♦ Allows the organization to build on what is already being done
♦ Aids in breaking down resistance to change
♦ Focuses on improved performance rather than budget figures
♦ Provides networking opportunities for employees that stimulate professional development
♦ Helps the assessments move out of the personal ownership realm and focus on an independent assessment level
♦ Helps eliminate wasted time and effort in rediscovery or nondiscovery of improved practices

♦ Gives the organization a proactive means of problem-solving performance issues.

Not everything should be benchmarked. Additionally, because one school performs an operation or activity better than
your organization, it still may not be the "best of the best."
Look for the "best of the best" before you implement the process so that changes initiated will result in "breakthrough" differences, not a series of "little bits." When considering benchmarking, refer to Shiba, Graham, and Walden (1993). They
warned: "Don't benchmark things that shouldn't be done at
all—you want to eliminate waste, not improve it!"

AFFINITY DIAGRAMS

All substantive implementation projects are likely to require some knowledge and/or skills that are new to the implementers. New programs in reading, math, science, office practices, custodial services, computer labs, media centers, and so
forth, must be assessed in terms of knowledge/skill requirements for implementers. Training to remove identified defi-
ciencies must be provided and the results documented. Expecting people to do that which they have not learned to do doesn't
make much sense. Affinity diagrams help identify needed
knowledge/skills for such projects. Affinity diagrams are tools
to use in identifying groups or categories of issues involved in
various implementation activities.

An affinity diagram, for example, might be used effectively
in identifying necessary training for implementing a new computerized student data information system. Individuals who
will be using the system could be asked to identify their top
three immediate training needs. Each of the identified needs
would be written on a separate card, post-it, slip of paper, or
any other kind of individual writing surface. Participants
should do this without interacting with others. The cards,
post-its, and so on, are collected and placed on a flat surface for
sorting. The individually identified training needs are sorted
into categories or problem topics. In this example of the new
computerized student data information system, the following
items might be submitted:

getting in to the system
what info is in there?

who can access the system?
checking security
coding
inputting data
sending info to another site
getting the midyear report done on this new system
printing reports
getting out of the system
accessing data
where can I get help?
do I need a new password?
logging on
will student I.D. be the same as before?
data input—how?
any new reports possible?
will GPAs be automatically figured?
is there a backup system?
how will current data be put into the new system?
when will the complete switch be made?
data entry—how?
what report formats are available?

Once these items are assembled in one place, the process of organizing and reorganizing them into categories begins. The separate sheets or cards can be grouped and regrouped as categories are created and collapsed. This categorizing and recategorizing would continue until such time as the needs seemed to have been grouped in such a way that both identification of what training needs are required and the general numbers of individuals needing them are displayed. The categories with the most individual items clustered in them would indicate those training areas in greatest demand. Based on these groupings, the three priority areas could be identified, and an overview of the topics which implementers perceive a need to learn could surface. Additionally, issues for the future can be prioritized.

Another example of affinity diagram use relates to information to be included in a parent/student handbook. Through a variety of mechanisms including phone calls, small group meetings, large group meetings, office visits, parent conferences, and tracking of phone call questions received, parents can be asked to identify what questions they have about school procedures or what information they would like to see in the parent/student handbook. As responses are received, they are grouped and regrouped into categories of topics and questions. As the clusters begin to emerge, they may be used to develop a new document or as a template for assessing what changes are needed in an existing document to better address the information needs of the intended audience.

Use of affinity diagrams allows the receivers of the document to express what they want to know as well as allowing the senders of the document to decide what it is they want the receiver to know. According to Lewis and Smith (1994), the affinity diagram "organizes pieces of information into groupings based on the natural relationships that exist among them" (p. 97).

This tool provides an easy means of getting large numbers of individuals involved in a process of identifying what changes might be needed and strategies for implementing them. As always, when and with whom to use this tool must rely on the quality judgment of the knowledgeable and skilled principal.

STAGES OF CONCERN QUESTIONNAIRE

The Stages of Concern Questionnaire (SoCQ) can help principals identify the concerns that individuals have regarding a particular change. The SoCQ proposes that individuals progress through seven stages of concerns as users or potential users of an innovation (Figure 3.3). Each Stage has a "cluster" of concerns that if known regarding an individual or a group, can provide guidance in giving appropriate assistance to them. For example, those whose greatest concerns are at Stages 1 and 2 want to know more about the proposed change and how it will affect them. Concerns at Stage 3 focus on the logistics of implementing the proposed change, while those at Stages 4 and 5 center on the impact the proposed change will have on students and working collaboratively with others.

Different strategies are needed to address each concern level and move the individual or group to the next developmental point. According to Hord, et al. (1987), "concerns can be a highly effective guide to actions that school leaders might take to facilitate the implementation of change" (p. 43). For example, Pankake and Palmer (1996) described how they used the SoCQ to identify what changes were needed to help teachers imple-

FIGURE 3.3. STAGES OF CONCERN: TYPICAL EXPRESSION OF CONCERN ABOUT THE INNOVATION

		Stages of Concern	Expression of Concern
I	6	Refocusing	I have some ideas about something that would work even better.
M			
P	5	Collaboration	I am concerned about relating what I am doing with what other instructors are doing.
A			
C			
T	4	Consequence	How is my use affecting kids?
T			
A	3	Management	I seem to be spending all my time getting material ready.
S			
K			
S	2	Personal	How will using it affect me?
E	1	Information	I would like to know more about it.
L	0	Awareness	I am not concerned about it (innovation).
F			

Reproduced by permission from Southwest Educational Development Laboratory, Austin, TX (Hord, Rutherford, Huling-Austin, & Hall, 1987). *Taking Charge of Change*, Austin, TX: SEDL and ASCD (p. 31).

ment full inclusion of disabled students in their classrooms. The concerns that kindergarten teachers' revealed on the SoCQ about including students with severe multiple disabilities in their regular classrooms were used to determine what staff development strategies might be most effective in implementing this practice. As the concerns changed over the life of the project, staff development strategies did, too. The strategies were changed to address the teachers' concerns; that is, the tool (SoCQ) provided information upon which to determine needed changes.

The SoCQ can easily be used to assess concerns related to any innovation being introduced such as block scheduling, staff teaming, inclusion of students with special needs, new computer hardware and/or software, consolidation of two schools, opening of a new school, introduction of a new curriculum, use of new teaching materials, use of new instructional strategies, use of a peer coaching model, or implementation of a new teacher induction program. The group or individual concerns expressed through the SoCQ provide information upon which to base actions. For example, if the majority of mentor teachers in the new teacher induction program are expressing management concerns regarding the program, some action needs to be taken to assist them in developing strategies for organizing their time, schedules, and workloads. Additional awareness and informational sessions on mentoring and induction programs would be viewed by the implementers as useless and raise barriers to their implementation efforts rather than offer assistance.

The SoCQ is a 35-item, pencil-and-paper instrument that takes about 15 minutes to complete. The information from the instrument can be used to develop profiles that show the intensity of concern at each of seven levels for individuals or groups. Interpretation of the profiles requires some practice. A manual and permission to use the SoCQ are available from the Southwest Educational Development Laboratory in Austin, Texas. A similar instrument has also been developed to assess the concerns of change facilitators, those individuals who assist the implementers of an innovation. The Change Facilitator Stages of Concern Questionnaire or CFSoCQ (Hall, Newlove, George, Rutherford, & Hord, 1991) is completed by the change facilitators and provides the information necessary for developing profiles of their concerns. As with the SoCQ, the intensity of areas of concerns can be identified and appropriate supportive actions taken.

IMPLEMENTATION CONFIGURATION MATRIX

The Implementation Configuration Matrix (ICM) was developed as a tool to help individuals "talk about an educational program in clear, operational terms" (Hord et al., 1987, p. 13). The matrix displays the variations of use patterns that occur as implementers put components of a new program or change efforts into operation. These variations of the use patterns can then be assessed as "ideal," "acceptable," or "unacceptable."

Components are the "major operational features" or "parts" of the program/innovation and usually involve materials, teacher behaviors, and student activities (Hord et al., 1987). Identifying the components and their variations in use is a complex task that requires training and practice. The resulting matrix, however, will help clarify expectations for those who must implement the program/change effort.

The sample matrix shown in Figure 3.4 (pp. 58–59) was developed at the Southwest Educational Development Laboratory (SEDL) in Austin, Texas. The innovation, cooperative learning as an instructional strategy, is described through the six components of teacher behavior that are essential to implementing this instructional strategy. Each of the components is then described in terms of the variations that might appear in classrooms as implementation efforts get underway. The variation(s) to the left of the dotted line drawn from component 1 through component 6 are acceptable. When these variations of the components are operating in a classroom, then the innovation (here, cooperative learning), is being successfully implemented. Certainly, some components may move into the acceptable range of implementation while others do not. The goal, however, is to continue to work with the innovation and those attempting to implement it until all variations are ideal or at least acceptable as described on the ICM.

The ICM can help in evaluating any implementation project or program. The components and variations provide a template for assessing whether or not current efforts mirror those described in the ideal and/or acceptable variations on the ICM. Whenever one or more components in practice fall outside the acceptable variations on the matrix, changes are needed. Additionally, developing an ICM can be a powerful exercise in moving individuals to talk in specifics about exactly what will be happening when successful implementation has occurred. Having discussions about what teachers will be doing when they are members of a learning community, or exactly what it is that students who are technologically literate do, or just what materials and activities do we mean when we reference interdisciplinary curriculum, moves definition from the global to the more particular. This, in turn, helps people begin to assess where they are currently in relationship to where they want to be in the future. The distance between these two points becomes the target for change.

FIGURE 3.4. IMPLEMENTATION CONFIGURATION MATRIX ON COOPERATIVE LEARNING MATRIX

The Teacher:

Component 1: Structures Groups

(1)	(2)	(3)	(4)	(5)
Assigns students to 4-member groups	Assigns students to work with a partner	Assigns students to groups larger than 4		Does not assign students to groups

Component 2: Structures Tasks

(1)	(2)	(3)	(4)	(5)
Explicitly defines tasks and criteria for success as all group members accomplishing the task	Explicitly defines tasks and criteria for success as most group members accomplishing the task	Explicitly defines tasks and criteria for success as some group members accomplishing the task	Specifies no criteria for success	Specifies no task

Component 3: Assure Individual Accountability

(1)	(2)	(3)	(4)
Selects any or all group members to answer for the group and/or give individual tests to each student	Repeatedly selects those who typically answer correctly	Fails to solicit answers from ethnic/minority students or from girls	Permits one student to complete tasks and answer for the group

Component 4: Develops Group Skills

(1)	(2)	(3)	(4)	(5)
Explicitly states, monitors, and rewards group or social skills expected during the task	States and monitors group skills expected to be exhibited	States but does not monitor or reward expected group skills	Does not state, monitor, or reward group or social skills	

Component 5: Promotes Positive Interdependence

(1)	(2)	(3)	(4)	(5)
Consistently arranges (organizes) tasks so that group members must depend on one another to complete the task	Frequently arranges (organizes) tasks so that group members must depend on one another to complete the task	Occasionally arranges (organizes) tasks so that group members must depend on one another to complete the task	Arranges tasks that permit group members to complete the task alone	

Component 6: Develops Skills to Analyze and Assess the Group Processing

(1)	(2)	(3)	(4)	(5)
Provides students time and procedures to analyze how well they are using the necessary social skills	Continues to enhance analysis and assessment skills	Monitors the students' development of group process analysis and assessment	Allows students to analyze and assess how their groups function	Does not give attention to analysis and assessment of group processing

.... Variations to the right are unacceptable; variations to the left are acceptable
_____ Variations to the left are ideal

Example of a completed ICM taken from the *Leadership for Change Materials* developed and disseminated by the Southwest Educational Development Laboratory, Austin, TX. (Reproduced with permission.)

PROJECT PLANNING OR PROJECT MANAGEMENT PLANNING

A tool that can assist in identifying and initiating needed changes is commonly called project planning or project management. This tool helps coordinate the tasks, time, and costs for components or phases of change efforts. The resulting document is called a project plan. It is especially useful in organizing one-time projects that have clear starting and ending points. Lewis (1991) defines project management as "the planning, scheduling, and controlling of project activities to achieve performance, dollar, and time objectives for a given scope of work" (p. 6). The overall responsibility of the plan belongs to the project manager; however, a group of people, or project team, work with the project manager in developing, implementing, and monitoring the plan. Using project management helps with identifying strategies for change; additionally, it can help generate ownership by getting those who must implement the change directly involved in planning and developing strategies for its accomplishment. Using a project planning form is helpful for developing the "Work Breakdown" (Lewis, 1991) scheme for project goals.

A modified form allows identification of the goal, missions, and tasks. Additionally, responsibility and timelines can be added. Both of these additions are helpful for monitoring progress and establishing checkpoints. Responsibility identifies with whom to check for completion and the timeline identifies when the activities are to be completed. This stage of development is an excellent opportunity to coordinate tasks and involve others. Using some of the strategies described in the next chapter is helpful here. The sample form that follows (Figure 3.5) has been used by school districts in the implementation of school improvement efforts. This form includes information on what the project is to accomplish, who has responsibility for managing the project, who serves on the project team, what the major missions and tasks involved in the project are, and who will do them and when. It does not include the cost estimates, but these could easily be added if needed. While this example deals with student performance, project plans can also be developed for the implementation of processes.

Similar to the Business Process Mapping, Project Planning can be employed using a pencil and paper or computer software specifically designed for this purpose.

FIGURE 3.5. EXAMPLE OF A STUDENT
PERFORMANCE PROJECT PLAN

Project Goal: By May, students in grades 3, 4, and 5 will demonstrate
proficiency in Language Use by scoring an average of 84%,
79%, and 81%, respectively, on the Language Survey.
Project Manager: Anita
Project Staff: Rita, Vern, Craig, Darrell, Jill, and David

Missions & Tasks	Operating Responsibility	Due Date
1.0 Form teacher committees	Anita	9/1
1.1 Select grade level and area committee reps	Project Staff	(8/10)
1.2 Establish meeting schedule	Project Staff	(8/10)
2.0 Secure correct teaching tools		
2.1 Correlate language objectives with text & teaching materials		
2.2 Identify supplement materials		
2.3 Purchase supplements		
3.0 Set quarterly student performance targets		
3.1.........		

PERFORMANCE PROBLEMS FLOWCHART

In 1970, Robert Mager and Peter Pipe wrote *Analyzing Performance Problems or "You Really Oughta Wanna"* (Mager and Pipe's *Analyzing Performance Problems* is currently published by Kogan Page in London). The book describes a way to identify and analyze problems where there is a discrepancy between an individual's actual performance of a job compared to the desired performance of that job. Through the use of a series of questions presented in a flowchart format, Mager and Pipe lead principals through the steps of the analysis process. By responding to each of the steps, problems are identified and possible solutions generated. There also are questions to help with the selection of the best solution. The book presents detailed information on each of the steps in the analysis process. Additionally, a quick-reference checklist is provided.

Mager and Pipe's (1970) work reveals the importance of accurately identifying the problem prior to applying any solutions. The book has a number of examples of what can happen when solutions and problems don't match. Expending resources to apply ideal answers before the real questions have been identified is wasteful. Most common among the solutions applied in various situations is to send individuals to training. Mager and Pipe (1970) emphasize that individuals who are not performing as desired may know how to perform as expected but something in the environment prevents them from doing what is expected. Mager and Pipe assert that, as a result of these environmental factors, sending the person to training is unlikely to change performance unless the environment in which the individual works also changes. This perspective is similar to the quality principle of improving the system in order to improve performance. As Walton (1986) noted, "Workers work within a system that—try as they might—is beyond their control. It is the system, not their individual skills, that determines how they perform" (p. 51). The tools developed by Mager and Pipe assist principals in identifying problems in the system that, when solved, will improve the performance of individuals. This helps principals use limited resources more efficiently and effectively by aligning problems and solutions before taking action.

SUMMARY

The tools described in this chapter are only a few of those available. Time should be allotted to study these tools and locate others that may be of particular use with specific programs and change efforts.

When making your choice(s) it is wise to check with individuals who have used specific tools successfully. Doing so will save time and energy, as well as help align tools with tasks.

FOLLOW-UP ACTIVITIES

1. Consider the statement by Lippett, Langseth, and Mossop on the first page of this chapter. Determine its validity regarding you and your professional staff?

2. Select at least two of the tools described in this chapter (Force-Field Analysis, Change Potential Analysis Chart, Business Process Mapping, Benchmarking, Affinity Diagram, Stages of Concern Questionnaire(s), Performance Problems

Flow Chart, Implementation or Configuration Matrix, and Project Planning) and apply them to projects currently underway or ones under consideration. Use the information gained from the application of the tools to make corrective adjustments on current projects or to help develop implementation plans for new initiatives.

3. Develop a matrix or pictorial history of change in your school or school district. Identify the various change initiatives in the organization over a specific time period (e.g., 5 years, a decade, 20 years, since the school's opening, etc.). Trace the development of each initiative from start to final status. For some projects the history may be short, with a fate that did not include implementation or continuation. For others the history may be traced to the present day as a process, program, or project still in use. Once the overview of the history of change in your school or school district is evident, try to analyze what helped some initiatives succeed and/or what caused others to fail. Involving your school leadership team and/or the entire staff in this project is encouraged.

4

FACILITATING COORDINATION AND COLLABORATION OF TASKS

THE PEOPLE COMPONENT OF IMPLEMENTATION

Organizations require people to make them work. Schools are organizations. There would be no schools if there were not people to attend them, to work in them, and to support them. Conversely, people create organizations to help them more easily and effectively work together to achieve common goals. The structure of an organization is intended to enable people to achieve these goals by helping them know what to do, how to do it, and whether or not they are in fact achieving those common goals, while providing the necessary resources for accomplishment.

Structures that support and enhance the performance of individuals and groups in the school are essential. Additionally, ways must be found to help people understand how their individual efforts contribute to the achievement of organizational goals. Individuals and groups in the school must work together in a coordinated manner to make things happen, that is, to implement. Facilitating this coordination and collaboration of tasks is an important aspect of implementation. Principals need to know about and be able to facilitate.

- ♦ What does it mean to facilitate?
- ♦ What knowledge and skills do principals need to be facilitators and help others be facilitators? (Are

there differences in facilitating the work of individuals and the work of groups? What knowledge and skills do principals need about groups and how they function? How can collaboration be encouraged?)

♦ What are some ways to ensure quality involvement? (What policies, procedures and practices can be created to help in coordinating the activities of the organization?)

These questions are the focus of this chapter.

WHAT DOES IT MEAN TO FACILITATE?

When principals facilitate the coordination and collaboration of tasks, they make it easier for implementation to occur. In this regard, Harvey (1990) states that, "Successful management is essential if we are to handle the complexities of our world, and simplicity facilitates success" (p. 5). He goes on with, "People can do something about ideas that are direct, straightforward, and simple. They can't implement ideas that most of us have trouble understanding. The more important the administrative domain, the more imperative it is to keep it simple" (p. 5). The perspective that Harvey presents should be taken to heart. Principals need to simplify whatever they can, whenever they can. "Keep It Short and Simple" (K.I.S.S.) has been offered as good advice for years. Principals interested in facilitating the coordination and collaboration of tasks will use this advice to guide their behavior. In general, to facilitate is to make "things" easier. For our purposes, it is to make implementation easier. Do not be misled by this seeming simplicity. Many well-intentioned facilitators do things that not only fail to make things easier, they create a climate of hostility and mistrust that effectively blocks subsequent efforts to provide implementers with needed assistance.

Making it easier to coordinate tasks is an important responsibility for principals. When the work being done in one area is in harmony with the work being done in other areas, things go more smoothly. Individuals work at the task rather than at trying to resolve conflicts, figuring out what went wrong and who is to blame, or arguing over who gets what resources. What are some of the actions that principals can take in helping this coordination to occur? Among the actions needed to facilitate the coordination and collaboration of tasks are:

- clarifying the tasks to be done
- providing resources for accomplishing the tasks
- ensuring that the appropriate people are involved in the planning and implementation of the tasks
- providing time for people to connect
- minimizing redundancies and overlaps in tasks
- creating completion timelines and "big picture maps" for viewing multiple projects simultaneously
- creating continuous feedback loops for evaluation and planning

Knowledge and skills from several domains must be brought together. Resulting actions cannot guarantee that everything will go smoothly; however, each of them helps the principal and others involved in the implementation process to think through and describe the necessary conditions for making things happen.

CLARIFY THE TASK

One of the principal's important responsibilities in facilitating coordination of tasks is to be sure that those responsible for carrying it out understand just what their task is. This seems so simple that it ought go without mention. However, Lewis (1991) credits the failure of many projects to what he calls a "ready–fire–aim" approach in which the push is to go ahead with doing something, whether or not it is what should be done. Similarly, Hamilton and Parker (1993) report that in a basic problem-solving procedure the first step of defining the problem is often skipped because it is "assumed that everyone already knows exactly what the problem is." Operating on that assumption can cause the loss of valuable time when recommended solutions don't fit with the variety of definitions held about the original problem. Defining the problem and each task, and being sure those responsible for doing it are clear about it, are worth the time it takes to do them.

Lewis (1991) suggests that the first step in any project is to make sure the problem is defined correctly. Principals can facilitate this for themselves and others by putting the problem to be addressed or the task to be accomplished in writing. Write it down, have others read and edit it, and gain agreement that "yes, this is what we are trying to accomplish." Spending time clarifying the problem/task at start helps focus the actions, time, and resources used in getting it done.

PROVIDE RESOURCES

Starting on a task only to find there are no resources for doing it can be frustrating, discouraging, and even anger-producing. Immediately upon defining the task, an estimate of "what it will take to get the job done" should be made. If the costs are too great, perhaps the task needs to be reevaluated: Should it be done at all? Can it be divided into smaller units for gradual completion? Do priorities need to be set on which tasks get the limited resources available? Being realistic in assessing what is needed to accomplish a task is important. In an earlier chapter, a commitment to long-term support was identified as a prerequisite for undertaking a change. At the implementation phase, tasks are the incremental units of the change process that must be completed for successful implementation to occur. Each of these tasks needs the commitment of necessary resources at the start to assure those doing the work that the school district's commitment is genuine.

GET THE RIGHT PEOPLE TOGETHER

Who should be involved in this work? Who are the important players? Are some individuals in need of information about what's going on but do not necessarily need to attend every planning and feedback session? Principals can facilitate the coordination of tasks by being sure that the right people are being brought together and informed about what is to be done, how it is being done, and their part in getting it done. Identifying whom to involve need not be a major production. For some projects merely asking who would like to be involved suffices. Other projects may require that individuals representing particular areas or points of view be directly or indirectly involved. This might be done by drafting a preliminary flowchart of the process and identifying which units are part of the process and which receive the outputs from the process. Another strategy is to identify core work groups and then involve others as needed through ad hoc groups. However it is accomplished, making sure that the right people get together is essential to successful implementation. The concept of a redundant (backup) system is particularly relevant here. Key people are exactly that—key. Loss of such a person can seriously interrupt, even stall, task completion. The impact on the total implementation project can be substantial.

PROVIDE THE TIME FOR PEOPLE TO GET TOGETHER

Once the right people are identified, they need the opportunity to get together. Time to talk and plan is important in coordination of tasks. Principals need to create ways to find time for the people involved in the tasks to get together. Times for people to get together should not always be before and after the work day. Providing some time during the workday makes a powerful statement about the importance of the work being done. Additionally, finding ways to get people together during the workday may increase their commitment to giving time outside the workday as well. Whether it is during the workday or volunteer time, getting together to interact is critical. This is true not only at the early stages of implementation but throughout the process. Being sure this time is available on an ongoing basis will keep implementation underway and provide the feedback loop important in preventing problems.

CREATE TIMELINES AND "BIG PICTURE" MAPS

Coordination of tasks implies that there are several tasks taking place at any one time. Helping people think through the sequence of events is an important planning skill. Additionally, checking with suppliers to be sure they can meet the identified timelines is important. The intent is to get a sense of what needs to be done, by whom, and when. Additionally, it avoids having an overload of things due at one point and also identifies what tasks are prerequisites for the completion of others.

Creating a timeline or "big picture" map can be accomplished in a variety of ways and at differing levels of sophistication. Placing all of the tasks and their due dates on a master calendar will help everyone see the things happening during any one month, how many tasks are prerequisite to completion of others, and so forth. A simple "things to do" list brain-stormed by the work groups and then sequenced for completion can serve the purpose in most situations. However, planning and scheduling tools such as PERT and Gantt Charts can also assist with creating timelines and "big picture" maps of multiple tasks. These tools can be used to monitor results.

Principals certainly need to encourage the creation of time-lines and "big picture" maps for any new project that is initiated in the school. Timelines and "big picture" maps should also be done for current, ongoing projects. Doing this helps bring realistic thinking to just how much is going on in the school at any one time—current and new. Realizing what tasks are necessary to maintain current projects can avoid over commitment of time, energy, and resources to new projects. Whether a simple list or a sophisticated charting tool, seeing the "big picture" is an important strategy in facilitating the coordination and collaboration of tasks for successful implementation.

IDENTIFY OVERLAPS AND REDUNDANCIES

Two or three people doing the same thing while another task goes unattended is a situation to be avoided. Be sure that each task has someone who is responsible for doing it. Having the sequence of who needs to be doing what choreographed so they connect but not overlap and making sure things move toward completion are important in facilitating the coordination of tasks. Using the business process mapping (BPM) tool presented in Chapter Three will be helpful in identifying who is doing what and when. Defining what inputs are needed prior to action, what outputs are produced by the actions taken, and if these outputs are needed as inputs for the next task are important activities in avoiding overlaps and redundancies. Seeing the connection of one set of actions as prerequisites (or inputs) to the next set of actions is important to effective coordination. Being connected without being redundant is the balance needed.

CREATE A FEEDBACK LOOP

Take care that getting things done does not overlook checking to see that things are going well. Being busy is not necessarily being productive. Some mechanisms must be developed to provide feedback information about what is happening so that adjustments can be made as needed. These mechanisms might include face-to-face meetings with those involved, a recorded feedback hotline, or periodic updates of the project plan/"to do" list. When decisions to adjust are made, they need to be shared with everyone involved. Each decision to adjust may in turn require that other adjustments be made. Keeping the information flowing to those who need it is important for both performance and attitude. Additionally, failure to provide information can cause individuals to doubt the sincerity of those directing the work. Creating feedback loops then becomes a means for facilitating positive attitudes as well as task completion.

These seven guidelines are examples of actions that principals should exercise in facilitating the coordination and collaboration of tasks. Actions need to be properly sequenced. Some are prerequisites to planning, others are best applied during planning stages, and still others must be repeated periodically as work gets underway. Every situation has unique features that will need to be assessed in relation to what actions will best make things happen. Developing a variety of possible actions for use as needed would be wise.

WHAT KNOWLEDGE AND SKILLS DO PRINCIPALS NEED TO BE FACILITATORS AND HELP OTHERS BE FACILITATORS?

The most comprehensive answer to this question involves all 21 of the NPBEA knowledge and skills domains. For example, skills in leadership, motivating others, and delegation are all involved in successfully facilitating and helping others be successful facilitators. More specifically, to effectively facilitate implementation principals should be skilled in areas such as:

- ◆ listening
- ◆ questioning
- ◆ anticipating and predicting
- ◆ persistence and patience
- ◆ identifying and reducing resistance
- ◆ securing resources
- ◆ working with groups

LISTENING

Hoy and Miskel (1996) point out that listening skills are necessary if "relatively accurate, two-way exchanges" are to occur. Myriad exchanges will take place as the tasks of implementation get underway. Principals can enhance their success in facilitating the coordination and collaboration of tasks by becoming skilled listeners. Listening is a skill. Unfortunately, many of us have had little formal training in developing it; yet, listening makes up at least half of all communication time (Bone, 1988). Effective listening can help principals collect information about how things are going and assist in understanding the concerns of others.

According to Hamilton and Parker (1993), "Listening to employees is a way of showing support and acceptance, which make for a more open climate, and an open climate makes employee satisfaction and productivity more likely" (p. 111). They go on to identify three "payoffs of effective listening":

- ◆ it is a method of discovering the values, needs, expectations and goals of others;
- ◆ it helps better relationships develop between individuals when each is listening to the other; and,
- ◆ it provides an opportunity for others to learn from their experiences so that we copy their successes and avoid their mistakes.

Similarly, Bone (1988) states that "Those who know how to listen can better understand problems, sustain attention, retain information, [and] improve working relationships" (p. 4). A strong case can be made for increasing skills in this area. Recommendations for improving an individual's listening skills are available. Written materials, video- and audiotape programs, courses, and workshops for improving communication skills generally and listening skills specifically are offered by a variety of business and educational organizations. For example, Bone (1988) offers "Ten Tips for Tip-Top Listening," which includes taking notes, setting positive expectations, really wanting to listen, and creating an environment in which few or no distractions are present. Similarly, Hunsaker (1983) provides readers with a set of activities to help them analyze their listening skills, identify why they listen, and keep a diary of how much listening they do and to whom. These resources are only a few of the many available for learning how to change bad habits and develop new ones that will result in improved skills as a listener.

Principals skilled in listening are more accurate in receiving and sending information important to the success of the implementation efforts. Helping others develop listening skills to increase the accuracy of their exchanges facilitates the coordination of tasks as well.

QUESTIONING

Skill in asking questions can be of great assistance to principals in facilitating the coordination and collaboration of tasks. For some time leaders were seen as problem-solvers, individuals who "had the right answers." Now leaders are more likely to be seen as individuals who ask and help others to ask "the right questions." Skill in posing questions can help self and others focus without demanding a predetermined response. The use of effective questioning skills can help others to become more able in identifying problems and seeking solutions rather than expecting the principal to do this work.

Kouzes and Posner (1987) claim that questions not only help focus issues and concerns, but they can "point people in the 'right direction'." They suggest that the questions that the leader asks send messages about the organization's focus, provide feedback about which values should be attended to, and indicate the amount of energy that should be devoted to each. They assert that "...it is readily apparent that the leader's questioning style has a pervasive effect on the issues that organizational members worry about" (p. 203).

Another illustration of questioning as an important skill is found in Mager and Pipe's book *Analyzing Performance Problems* (1984). Each phase of the analysis of performance problems is initiated by posing and responding to a series of questions. The questions focus the analysis, identify what information to gather, and provide guidance regarding what to look for in that information once it has been gathered. Questions provide the framework for analysis. The same questions are appropriate to ask in different situations whereas solutions or answers to the situations may differ greatly.

There are a variety of question types, each having a different purpose. Individuals in the fields of communication, leadership, supervision, management, and counseling have studied and written about skilled questioning. For example, Hamilton and Parker (1993) identified three types of problem solving questions: fact, value, and policy. Each type of question requires a different focus and strategy for obtaining a relevant response:

- Questions of fact need a valid research strategy and their purpose is to determine whether something is fact.

- Questions of value require personal judgment regarding the worth or desirability of something.

- Questions of policy rely on both research and judgment. Responses to policy questions generally require a specific change in process or action thus changing the way things have been done.

Earlier, Kirby (1980) sorted questions for use by supervisors into four types: opportunity, problem-oriented, expanding, and narrow:

- Opportunity questions are open-ended, thus giving myriad response possibilities: "How are things going with the project?" or "What have we learned in these first few weeks of our effort to implement this?"

- Problem-oriented questions focus on a specific situation or problem and help generate information about how to deal with or solve it: "Specifically, what should be done to take care of this?" or "How do you plan to handle it?"

- Expanding questions are asked to develop information in a more limited area: "What are your suggestions for solving this conflict?" or "What will be your strategy for getting this done?" The area is limited, but the question expands the information available about that particular area.

♦ Finally, the most restrictive questions are called "narrow." The possible responses are few and may often be limited to "yes" or "no": "Are we ready to proceed?" or "Can that be addressed in the council meeting?"

Practicing what questions to ask, when to ask them, and to whom to direct them helps develop these skills. Principals who are skilled in questioning will make more efficient and effective use of their time and the time of others. As asking the right questions becomes routine, everyone, not just principals, will begin to use this strategy in their initial planning and problem solving. Making this a general practice will facilitate the coordination and collaboration of tasks for successful implementation.

ANTICIPATING AND PREDICTING

Skills in anticipating and predicting all kinds of things—behavior, feelings, results, resource needs, consequences, and so forth—are important for facilitating the coordination and collaboration of tasks. Synonyms for "anticipate" and "predict" include expect, foresee, forecast, and envision, and the definitions include "to feel or realize beforehand," "act in advance so as to prevent," "to state or tell about in advance." While these may seem more like skills for psychics, they are, in fact, important skills for principals seeking to achieve successful implementation.

Anticipating and predicting are the skills that help principals and those with whom they work guard against "Murphy"! Almost everyone knows Murphy's Law; they laugh about and often assert they are victims of it. However, hardly anyone plans for it! The one way to guard against Murphy is to become skilled in anticipating and predicting.

Strategies to help principals anticipate and predict are numerous. One example is the advice Bridges (1991) gives in his book *Managing Transitions*. He admonishes us to "foresee as much as you can" (p. 73). He recommends doing "worst-case scenarios" by building in a "what if clause" to every plan. Bridges said, "The only way to prepare for the unexpected is to build into all of your plans a contingency clause that specifies what you will do if the unexpected happens" (p. 75). By doing this, alternative routes are ready for use if (according to Murphy, when) something does go wrong. For example, if a project requires training for successful implementation to occur, what would happen if:

♦ the individual(s) to conduct the training can't be located?, or

♦ an ice-storm occurs the night before the training is scheduled?, or

♦ the training proves to be ineffective?, or

♦ the copy center can't get the training materials reproduced in time for distribution?, or

♦ the materials arrive in sufficient number and on time, but are out of order and some pages are not readable?

Here is another example to illustrate the power of doing a "worst-case scenario." What would happen if:

♦ a key individual in the project takes another position or experiences a sudden illness?, or

♦ the space allocated for use is suddenly needed for a different (but priority) use?, or

♦ a committee of parents or other concerned citizens initiates expressions of concern regarding the intent and processes involved?

Asking "what if" must not paralyze the process. Taken to the extreme, individuals could spend all of their time identifying what could go wrong and never get started on anything. On the other hand, to assume that everything will go exactly as planned is foolish. Asking "what if" is worthy of adopting as a routine practice. Being realistic without becoming pessimistic is the balance to achieve. Principals must become skilled at this and model this skill for others.

While Bridges' recommendation deals with "worst-case scenarios," predicting consequences in the opposite direction is also important. Deciding how to handle situations of success also requires prediction and anticipation skills. Managing the positive consequences of a project can be important. For example, what if we succeed in:

+ coaching the team to a winning season and they move into the playoffs?, or

+ developing students who are critical thinkers and they begin to question and criticize the organizational structure?, or

+ increasing the quality of mathematics instruction so much that more students' elect higher level math courses than there is staff to teach them?, or

+ helping teachers become so skilled in curriculum and instructional adaptations for special needs students that special education referrals drop dramatically?

Each of these examples describes accomplishments we would embrace. On the other hand, achieving them requires that we be ready and able to make adjustments to accommodate and sustain them. Principals should spend time working with the "what if" scenarios of success as well as those for "worst-cases." In addition to planning, talking through such possibilities could uncover some sources of resistance to the overall project.

Skills in anticipating and predicting are proactive rather than reactive. They are needed if principals are to look beyond the now. Principals who are looking ahead and planning for what might happen are facilitating. They are making it easier to successfully implement. They ask many questions and encourage others to do the same. They look for someone to play the devil's advocate so they can see the worst. They recall what happened last time and use it as a lesson in planning for this time. They consult with individuals who have roles and responsibilities for the success of the tasks. They use their skills in listening and questioning to help gather the very important information needed for predicting and anticipating. Additionally, they do this work with others. By engaging in these activities, they not only use their skills in anticipating and predicting, they model and teach these skills to others.

PERSISTENCE AND PATIENCE

Implementation takes time. Having a wealth of patience and persistence serves principals well as they seek to facilitate and help others become facilitators. It is important to recall that a prerequisite to implementation is a long-term commitment. Before beginning a project, knowing it will take time and ongoing support is essential. But even when we are on a trip we want or need to take, we can become tired and discouraged. Therefore, patience and persistence must be among the skills that principals possess and use in assuring that successful implementation occurs.

Patience and persistence must be modeled by the principal if they are to be expected from others. If the leader gives up, what keeps others focused? If the leader gets discouraged, what brings hope to others? If the leader is unwilling to try again or try something different, how can others be expected to persist?

This is not to suggest that principals are void of normal human feelings. The intent is to emphasize that what the principal does and does not do has a pervasive influence on the other persons involved. Because principals are people, too, they are expected and allowed to have the same feelings as everyone else. They need, however, to monitor when, where, to whom, and at what level these feelings are expressed. A certain level of anxiety, discouragement, and impatience is important to express in helping others see the human side of the leader. A certain level of comfort can be derived from seeing that "the principal knows how we feel" and/or "even the principal admits this is harder than we thought it might be."

Principals need a network of peers to whom such feelings can be openly expressed. A peer group experiencing similar ups and downs in their schools provides a forum for venting feelings while gaining needed support, encouragement, and understanding to strengthen commitment to continue.

Another strategy is to visit an organization where the particular program is already in place. Sometimes seeing in reality just what you are trying to achieve can restore enthusiasm and determination. Yet another suggestion is to attend a professional development activity focused on the particular area being implemented. Many of the national and state level professional associations offer institutes that focus on specific topics. Using a variety of electronic sources to access networking groups and professional development opportunities should be explored. Bulletin boards and conversation groups on all kinds of topics are available through Internet. Interactive video and satellite conferences and professional development activities are increasing. When time and money are at issue (and they usually are) these technology options can be cost-effective.

Perhaps the most important recommendation for principals when discouragement abounds is to visit your school's classrooms. Talking with students about their hopes and dreams can reinforce why you initiated the program or project. Seeing just who is to benefit from successful implementation efforts serves as a powerful energizer.

While each of these strategies is specifically offered to principals, they are also applicable to everyone involved in the implementation effort. Networks, site visits, and professional development activities can help everyone involved to be patient and persistent. As in so many areas of life, you can't help anyone else until you help yourself. While providing these boosts for others is important, providing them for yourself may be even more important. Principals are key in setting the tone for the school. Making sure your capacity to persist and be patient is unending is the best strategy for assuring the adoption of these characteristics by others.

IDENTIFYING AND REDUCING RESISTANCE

"Not all changes are fun and not everyone has fun changing" (Shelley, 1995). Implementing a change or program innovation often generates resistance. Efforts to make things easier (facilitate) can go a long way toward reducing the resistance that arises during implementation. People resist changing for a variety of reasons, none of which really have to make sense to anyone but the resister. To reduce an individual's resistance, you have to realize they are resisting and identify the source of that resistance. Gaining skill in identifying resistance, analyzing its source, and developing strategies for reducing it is important for principals as facilitators.

There are several good references that address sources of resistance. Among them are E. Mark Hanson (1991), Thomas Harvey (1990), and Michael Fullan (1991). The following are some of the sources of resistance that have been identified by these and other authors. Each is presented by name, a basic description or definition is given, and then suggested approaches to reduce the intensity of the resistance are offered:

+ Fear of the unknown.

Resistance often arises from a lack of clarity about
what exactly is going to happen and what an individual's role will be. Being as clear as possible
about what things will be like when the program or
process is fully implemented is crucial. Even if information was shared early on, repetition of this information is important. Continuous descriptions
of the long-range view and the short-term actions
help give people a sense of security. Conversations
about the vision alternated with specifics regarding the next steps to move ahead may help reduce
the fear of the unknown.

+ Vested interests.

A vested interest is a source of resistance when individuals or groups have a personal or professional stake in keeping things the way they are. If
someone's job will be eliminated or a program
from which a parent's child has benefited is threat-
ened, a natural reaction is to try and keep things
the way they are. In response, principals need to
identify ways in which these people can become
vested in the new program or processes by describing the new roles to be played or identifying the
ways in which current benefits will be maintained
or even improved with the new program or processes.

+ Lack of incentives.

This refers to the "what's in it for me" question that
everyone considers. Unlike businesses, schools are
rarely able to offer monetary incentives or added
benefits. However, recognitions and rewards that
can be offered include new colleagues, training,
group or individual planning time, and opportunities to teach others. Additionally, principals need
to assess the perceived sacrifices and/or risks involved in implementing any program or process
by talking with and listening to individuals who

express a willingness to "try." Diagnose what supports (fiscal, time, social, and psychological) they need to minimize their risks and maximize their gains. Then, act to provide it.

♦ Overload.

Overload occurs when there are numerous new initiatives happening in the school at the same time. When this occurs, people get confused about what is really important. They may even stop trying because they just can't handle "one more thing!" Being sensitive to this is important. Ways to reduce resistance from this source include identifying priority projects and actions, eliminating existing processes and projects that conflict with the new behaviors, and demonstrating what existing knowledge and behavior can be used with the new program or project.

♦ Contextual/organizational constraints.

There are a number of items that exist within a system that actively work against implementing changes. Hanson calls these sources of resistance "organizational." For example, high-stakes state testing can create resistance to implementing instructional strategies and curriculum enrichment because of the need to prepare for what is tested. Another example is trying to implement some sort of continuous progress learning system when the current organization is structured around specific grading periods and calendars. Principals need to identify system constraints. Requesting waivers of particular rules, adjusting internal policies, securing pilot status for a project, and blending new procedures with existing ones are among the strategies principals can use to minimize organizational constraints.

♦ Costs.

Costs for implementation can include time, energy, and space, as well as money. Securing needed resources of various kinds for the long-term is essential—a prerequisite for undertaking any process or project. Realistically identifying what is involved is important. Using the "worst-case scenarios" discussed earlier can help everyone better understand the many (and sometimes hidden) costs inherent in any implementation project. Periodic feedback to the participants and sponsors lets everyone know their efforts (costs) are paying off, which may be critical to continuing engagement. Memos or written plans that demonstrate long-term resource commitment build participants' confidence and may help them see changes as worth the costs and not just "this year's new thing."

◆ Dependent relationships.

Disruptions in social patterns can be disturbing. Proposing teaming to individuals who have worked independently, rearranging physical space where people have become comfortable, requiring individuals to work with relative strangers such as special consultants, individuals from central office, or even teachers who are only casual acquaintances, can generate resistance. Principals must help such aggregates of individuals develop a group identity and establish relationships and working parameters. Planning social as well as work opportunities for those involved might help foster a team spirit. Also, identifying how some things will stay the same even with the new program or process can provide a modicum of security for those resisting because of dependency relationships.

◆ Life stages.

People value different things at different points in their lives. Energy requirements, personal life responsibilities, and even willingness to commit to change vary with our experiences and stages of life. What appeals to someone in the early stages of their career may not be seen as meriting attention at a later career stage. Individuals with young families may have child care concerns, while those who just graduated the last child from college may not. Principals need to be keenly aware of the individual personal and professional life stages of those with whom they work. Diagnosing what different people want and need in their professional development is important for reducing resistance. This can be done by listening carefully to expressed concerns and making adjustments that assist with expressed needs.

♦ Lack of knowledge.

Sometimes, people just don't know how to do what it is that is supposed to be done. This is where staff development plays a crucial role in successful implementation. Staff development is not just presentations to increase awareness, but must include coaching and feedback. It is the principal's responsibility to insure that all elements of staff development are on-line as needed. Project staff must have time to talk about their work, to identify any emerging flaws, to redesign needed changes, and to gather and evaluate data regarding progress. This reduces or eliminates lack of knowledge as a source of resistance.

The sources of resistance reviewed here are a few from among the many that are possible. Each organization generates unique circumstances. It is important that we assess who is resisting and why. The resister may have some important point that needs to be considered, thought through, and acted on—if implementation is to succeed. As Carlson wisely noted, "To say all resistance is bad is to say that all changes are good." Rather than be angry that resistance occurs, principals who will be successful at implementation will see this as a natural consequence of change. It may even present opportunities to gain important insights for the ultimate success of the efforts.

SECURING RESOURCES

Successful implementation requires resources—human, physical, fiscal, and time. Fullan and Miles (1992) refer to change as being "resource hungry." Because resources are almost always limited and wants and needs seem always to be limitless, the skill of securing resources is crucial for facilitation. As noted earlier, a lack of resources can be a source of resistance. Adequate resources are key to the long-term success of the entire effort. Resource demands are unlikely to lessen when implementation occurs. In fact, the demands may increase.

Resources include everything and everyone. Knowing what resources are needed is an important first step in securing them. Just "getting things" may expend a lot of energy with few productive results. Learning how to determine resource needs and helping others develop this skill is important. Brainstorming with staff about what will be needed can be done by asking for the extreme situations: "At the most, what resources will be needed to do this?" and "What resources must we have as a minimum to get started?" Somewhere between these two extremes is a realistic estimate of needs.

Resources need to be sought everywhere—inside and outside the organization. Brainstorming "who might have…" and "where can we get…" ideas can be used early in the group's planning. Four kinds of actions—adding, reallocating, blending, and chunking—are offered as places to begin securing the necessary resources for implementation:

♦ Adding.

The ideal for securing resources is to be able to add to those that already exist. New resources can become available through an increase in general revenues, special project allocations, parent/teacher association gifts, interest from a school foundation, corporate sponsorship, and/or grants. Once the project or program to be implemented has been defined, an investigation of the funding sources should be conducted. All sources should be checked. A caution is appropriate, however: While grants and gifts can help at the beginning, planning for how the work will continue when these special funds are no longer available needs to be done early in the process. Many well-intended changes never became institutionalized because the "grant ran out." Looking ahead to plan for how new and continuing costs will be made part of the ongoing budget is important.

♦ Reallocating.

Oftentimes reallocation of existing resources may be more appropriate and readily available. This may be particularly true when referring to time, energy, personnel equipment, and space. The concept of "planned abandonment" is an important one to apply here by assessing where resources are currently being used for activities that are not adding value to the organization. Sometimes resources are being allocated to activities just because they have always been. A hard look is needed to see if these activities are really needed and if they are making a difference. If not, perhaps the resources can be reallocated to activities which are necessary to the new project or program.

♦ Blending.

What is already going on that could help support the new program or process? Finding some level of blend between what you want to have happen and what is already occurring could provide resources for the implementation efforts. Additionally, while you are securing resources for your own initiatives you are assisting others with their efforts. Not only can this be a resource assist, it helps generate advocacy for your project or program over the long-term.

♦ Chunking.

There is an old saying that the way to eat an elephant is "one bite at a time." That idea is applicable here. Principals are well-advised not to get themselves or the projects they are trying to implement into an "all or nothing" situation. Perhaps resources to support everything you want are not available. However, are there enough resources to help get started or to support some important component of the effort? If so, use them. When the positive results

of your efforts begin to materialize, you will be in a
stronger position to argue for additional resources.
Rather than wait for enough resources to do everything, identify a "chunk" of your project that can be
accomplished or started with the resources that can
be secured.

WORKING WITH GROUPS

Much of the work that goes into successful implementation
is dependent on the efforts of groups of individuals. Schools
are full of committees, councils, teams, and task forces. There
are groups to plan, to make decisions, to give advice, and to
evaluate. Many schools have grade-level groups, subject area
groups, fundraising groups, and instructional groups. What
happens in schools is influenced by teaching teams, academic
teams, athletic teams, booster clubs, and forensic leagues.
Work is accomplished and policies are developed through student councils, parent councils, site councils, advisory councils,
staff development councils, and discipline committees. Decision-making and responsibility for implementation are shared
with myriad others within the context of group work. Skills in
working with groups are essential if principals are to facilitate
successful implementation efforts.

There are both advantages and disadvantages to working
with groups rather than individuals. Hamilton and Parker
(1993) identified seven advantages:

- decisions jointly determined receive more support
  and commitment and result in less resistance to
  changes
- accuracy may be increased because more perspectives are taken into account prior to action being
  taken
- because decisions are likely to be better, they are
  more readily accepted by individuals outside the
  group
- when people are involved, their personal satisfaction is increased
- aggression and hostility are reduced

- ◆ productivity is increased
- ◆ more than one individual takes responsibility for the decision

This last advantage tends to diffuse the responsibility and spread both the credit and the blame, depending on the outcome. However, just doing things in groups doesn't guarantee that the quality of the outcomes is increased. Groups can exercise negative as well as positive influences.

According to Hamilton and Parker (1993), two characteristics define a group as being different from a collection of individuals: groups have some level of engagement in face-to-face interactions; and the members must be actively working toward a common goal. Identifying the right people and providing opportunities for those individuals to get together are means by which the principal can facilitate the first of these characteristics. The second characteristic requires different kinds of skills. According to Lunenburg and Ornstein (1996), "In the group decision-making process, decisions are the product of interpersonal decision processes and group dynamics. Thus, the school administrator must be concerned with leading the group from a collection of individuals to a collaborative decision-making unit" (pp. 162–63).

Some of the knowledge and skills that principals can use to develop collaborative units are establishing group norms, defining and assigning group roles and tasks, and providing a group-work process model to structure activities.

- ◆ Establishing group norms.

Principals can foster a collaborative environment for group work by establishing a set of "group norms." These are the rules for operating and interacting which the group members develop for themselves and agree to abide by throughout their work together. Developing these should be the first actions that the group takes. Group norms should:

- • be direct and specific in their guides for behavior
- • be written and posted (or handed out) at each work session

- be monitored and enforced by everyone in the group
- address all areas that are important for the group's work

Side conversations, for example, can be distracting and disruptive in the group. Therefore, one group norm might deal with this—no side conversations or comments will be allowed. More positively, the group might agree that "say it to the group" or "only one person speaks at a time." This encourages people to be polite and respectful; it reduces repetition because "someone wasn't listening"; and it helps create an open forum in the group. Another example of a group norm might be "to start on time and to stop on time." Given that time is a limited, nonrenewable resource, group members will appreciate efficient use of it. Because many meetings may be before or after the workday, members will be pleased to have start and stop times they can count on and plan around. Additionally, this rule may encourage individuals to be on time in order not to miss anything, and it may keep everyone focused on the business of the group, saving the "visiting" for other occasions.

These are some examples of the kinds of activities that group norms might address. While some items may be common between and among groups, each group should have the responsibility for creating its own set. Variations are necessary and depend on the individuals involved and the project or problem being addressed. Once established, however, the agreed upon norms must be observed by everyone in the group. In doing this, everyone in the group, not just the group leader, takes responsibility for the group operations and interactions.

♦ Defining and assigning group roles and tasks.

Once group norms are established, individual roles and task responsibilities should be defined and assigned. Everyone in the group has some responsibility for helping to get the work completed. The names, number, and specifics of roles and responsibilities needed for the group to function successfully vary based on the task at hand and the various subtasks that comprise it. This provides a framework for keeping the general purpose and its component parts in the appropriate relationship. The "leading and meeting" roles and responsibilities from the *DuPont Leadership Development Process Training* (1989), Hamilton and Parker's (1993) *Group Task and Maintenance Functions,* and Quick's (1992) *Team Building Roles* serve as examples of these lists of roles and responsibilities needed for groups to function effectively.

In the *DuPont Leadership Development Process Training* (1989) materials, the section on "Meeting Leading" identified four roles necessary for effective meetings: leader, resource, scribe, and participants. The leader focuses on the content of the meeting and is responsible for facilitating the work of the group and participation. The resource person helps the leader plan the meeting, monitors the processes of the group, assists with materials preparation and use, and intervenes if necessary to refocus the group on the purpose. It is the job of the scribe to listen carefully and record the information generated in the meeting. Finally, everyone in the group has the role and responsibility to serve as a participant by observing the operating rules and contributing positively to its purpose.

Hamilton and Parker (1993) offer two sets of roles and responsibilities necessary to effective functioning of a group: Group Task Functions and Group Maintenance Functions. Group Task Functions are needed for the group to accomplish its task and solve its problems. Among the Group Task Functions are:

- *Initiating*—offering ideas, solutions, procedures, and so forth to get the discussion started
- *Information giving*—offering data and experiences
- *Opinion seeking*—encouraging others to state their conclusions, judgments, beliefs, and attitudes
- *Elaborating*—expanding on ideas and suggestions
- *Energizing*—infusing the group with energy through their active involvement
- *Recording*—keeping a written record of activities and decisions

Maintenance Functions are those that contribute to the overall atmosphere and harmony of the group's work. Hamilton and Parker identified four Group Maintenance Functions:

- *Encouraging*—inviting active participation of everyone
- *Harmonizing*—setting a positive, agreeable tone for the interactions
- *Tension relieving*—infusing humor when tension builds
- *Gatekeeping*—keeping the group open for participation by everyone

Quick (1992) identified seven "team-building roles," which he says may be found consistently in teams that function effectively. These team-building roles include:

- *supporting*—providing support and encouragement to team members
- *confronting*—bringing attention to a team member's individual acts of behavior that may be generating hurt to others on the team .
- *gatekeeping*—monitoring to see that everyone has opportunity to participate and that no team member dominates
- *mediating*—intervening to arbitrate disputes between team members
- *harmonizing*—identifying areas of agreement when disagreements occur and inviting others to build on the identified areas of agreement
- *summarizing*—bringing together the various pieces of the discussion at intervals throughout the interactions
- *process observing*—gathering information at each meeting to provide feedback on the effectiveness of the processes used to determine if the processes are supports or impediments to the functioning of the group

Regardless of which list is used, the point is that for the group to be effective a variety of roles and responsibilities must be assumed and/or assigned. Training, practice, and feedback will serve best to make these a part of the work culture of the organization. Providing training in group process skills, assuring the opportunity for time to practice, and establishing feedback systems to inform performance improvement are the roles and responsibilities of the principal as the facilitative leader.

♦ Providing a group work process model

A group work process model should be established to provide structure for the conduct of activities within the group. Even with group norms and defined and assigned roles and responsibilities, some overall structures for doing the work of the group need to be in place. A traditional group decision-making/problem-solving model will provide this overall structure in most instances. Again, depending on the references used, the steps of the decision-making/problem-solving model will vary in number and name. However, most models will include some form of the following activities:

- *Define the problem or issue to be addressed.* Without some kind of definition of what is to be done the group will not know what they are to accomplish as a result of their work together. This step is a critical. Over 40 years ago, Peter Drucker (1954) cautioned leaders that "...there are few things as useless—if not as dangerous—as the right answer to the wrong question" (p. 353). Spending time determining the right question will save time in the long run.

- *Identify limitations, parameters, or evaluation criteria for the alternatives to be pursued.* This step of the process ensures that as much is known about the problem or situation as possible. Generating solutions prior to research and analysis of the problem or situation can result in such ineffective actions as dealing with symptoms rather than real problems; proposing solutions that will be rejected or are not feasible because of costs, legalities, and other limitations not considered; repeating recommendations tried previously; and creating divisions within the group that impede the work process.

- *Generate alternative solutions.* When the problem has been defined and researched, and the criteria established and set aside for use in the fourth step, the next task for the group leader is to provide an atmosphere in which group members feel free to generate numerous and creative alternatives to the problem or situation. No attempt should be made to critique the alternatives; that comes in the next step of the work process. Getting everyone involved and encouraging "possibilities thinking" are important to the group's work. Using methods such as brainstorming, nominal group technique, carousel brainstorming, and affinity diagrams encourages quality participation.

- *Evaluate alternatives generated.* The work of the group now shifts from development to evaluation. Each of the alternatives is referenced to each of the established criteria. Alternatives that do not meet the criteria are discarded. This process continues until each alternative has been evaluated in relationship to all of the established criteria. When this is completed, the large list of alternatives should be narrowed to only a few, or perhaps even a single alternative.

- *Select the best alternative.* If multiple alternatives for addressing the defined task result, then some mechanism to select the best alternative (or to prioritize or preference the alternatives) must be used.

- *Implement the alternative selected.* As the group process moves through each of the activity categories, the work of the group moves toward accomplishment. While the categories are not discrete and some issues may overlap from one category to another, they do have a general sequence to be followed and, in essence, are "steps" in structuring the process of group work.

Fullan (1991) noted that, "...implementation is doing, getting and supporting people who are acting and interacting in purposeful directions..." (p. 83). Establishing group norms, defining and assigning group roles and tasks, and providing a group work process model can help a group of individuals engage in the kinds of interactions which move them toward becoming a collaborative unit. Principals need knowledge and skills in working with groups if they are to facilitate rather than impede the coordination and collaboration of tasks for successful implementation.

WHAT ARE SOME WAYS TO ENCOURAGE QUALITY INVOLVEMENT?

An important element for creating ownership in the organization and its operations is to get people involved. Involving people, however, takes time—their time and the time for task completion. People don't want to give their time to involvement unless it makes a difference. On the other hand, involving everyone in everything regarding the operations of an organization, even if possible, runs the risk of bringing task completion efforts to a halt. The principal's responsibility is to create a balanced involvement that provides opportunities for participants to contribute in meaningful (as perceived by them) ways *and* allows the organization to operate efficiently and effectively. What is the balance between the two? How can members of the organization be involved in a quality way?

♦ Determine the level of involvement needed and desired.

Depending on the project or program underway, the need and desire for involvement will vary with the individuals from wanting "information" to "active participation." The level of involvement should ideally be determined by mutual agreement between the principal and the individual members. Criteria to be used in assessing the desired level might include:

- level of impact the program or project will have on the individual and the individual's work
- other commitments

- interest in the particular program or project being implemented
- level of knowledge and experiences needed for the project or program

Ideally, individuals who will be directly affected by the program, who are not already overloaded with other responsibilities and commitments, who have experiences and expertise that will be helpful, and who have a high level of interest in the work will be the most active participants. For example, if a high school is trying to implement a new instructional schedule, teachers who will be directly affected by that schedule need to be deeply involved. Some of these teachers might have some experience with alternative scheduling and would be good candidates for "active participation" on a task force or committee on the topic. Others might be interested but have other commitments that preclude their giving priority attention to a new instructional schedule and, therefore, would be less actively involved. These individuals certainly need information and should probably be consulted for input on a variety of issues regarding the scheduling project. Yet another group might be less directly affected by the schedule changes being considered. Their involvement would best be at the information level.

Another important technique for creating and maintaining quality involvement requires periodic assessment of the need/ desire to participate. Some individuals may only need information at one point in the implementation process, but later want or need a greater degree of active participation. The opposite may be true for someone who was actively involved initially, but whose need and desire for active involvement decreased after a time. Being sensitive to such changes will help maintain quality involvement. Wanting and needing to be actively involved but not being invited is discouraging, frustrating, and even anger-producing. Likewise, being expected to be interested in and actively involved in a program, project, or process for which you have little interest, expertise, or immediate need is also discouraging, frustrating, and anger-producing. Involving the individuals at the appropriate levels based on need and desire is an important means for encouraging quality involvement in successful implementation efforts.

♦ Model the involvement desired

Modeling the behavior desired from others is a powerful teaching tool. Principals who really want involvement from others will become the "walking/talking" epitome of involvement. They will be active, responsible group members. They will be regular attendees at group work sessions and not let other activities take priority. In groups, they will assume an active role though not always as the group leader. They will complete assigned tasks and report progress to the group. They will not seek to meet with others when those individuals have need to be in work group meetings. They may serve as the scribe or resource person and will accept one or more Task or Maintenance Functions. They will ask questions and be eager learners. They will expect no more of others than they expect from themselves. Seeing the organizational leader behaving in a committed, collaborative way will be important to others who have been asked to do the same.

♦ Make use of the talents and expertise of organizational members

Most organizations are rich with knowledgeable and talented members. Unfortunately, many organizations do not make use of this rich resource base. One means of encouraging quality involvement in implementation efforts is to invite individuals to provide a variety of knowledge and skills to support the projects, programs, and processes being implemented. While external agents can serve as excellent catalysts in getting things started in an organization, it is ultimately up to the members of the organization to make things happen; that is, to implement. It is through the use of the talents and expertise of the organization's members that successful implementation will occur—or not.

Being able to tap into the talents and areas of expertise of the people in your school requires that you know them. Principals should make a concerted effort to get acquainted with everyone in the organization to discover what talents and areas of expertise exist there. Reviewing résumés and personnel files for information on such areas as formal training, work experiences, specialized training, and licensing is a good place to start. Scheduling visits with each person to identify areas of professional interest, recreational interests and talents, hobbies, community service and involvement, group leadership skills, and career goals offers further information for matching individual talents and expertise with specific implementation efforts. Additionally, listening to the recommendations of others about who could be helpful in making things happen can be revealing about individuals' talents and expertise.

Inviting individuals to become involved in implementation efforts is a good strategy for encouraging quality involvement. Additionally, making use of the talent and expertise of these individuals is just plain smart. If we truly believe that people are our most important resource, then making optimum use of the people in our organization is one way of providing the resources needed for successful implementation.

◆ Make it easy to do

Make it easy to get involved. While most people like a challenge, few pursue the impossible. If getting involved is fettered with complications and long, drawn-out procedures, the process itself will limit the amount of quality involvement that occurs. Quality involvement will be limited if getting involved is perceived to be an "all or nothing" proposition rather than one which is flexible according to need and desire. Or, if getting involved always means getting more work to do, the anticipated consequences will limit quality involvement. If we really want people to become involved, we need to create ways to facilitate it, that is, make it easier.

For example, specifically describing the project, program, or process in clear terms, indicating the performance expectations of those working directly with the project, and including a best estimate of time commitment and duration of the project will help individuals screen themselves. Additionally, identifying a variety of involvement options that may require only a limited time-commitment, or that may be accomplished in an alternate setting, will encourage involvement. If quality involvement is desired, it must be encouraged, not punished. Making it easy to get involved and making a variety of involvement options available will help increase both the amount and quality of the involvement in implementation efforts.

◆ Recognize and reward involvement

People tend to do what gets noticed and rewarded. Principals need to create an environment in which quality involvement is noted and rewarded. One strategy that would support this need for recognition and reward is to give credit to all who help or will help with the efforts. Noticing the work of others can be a real influence on their staying involved and doing more. Being recognized is important to all of us. Recognition can be verbal; it might also be in written form such as in the school newsletter, a memo, or a personal note.

Using members of the group to do presentations and to teach and tell others about the project encourages quality involvement. Principals can give center stage to the group members and spotlight them when reporting progress of the implementation efforts or doing workshops and presentations. When members of the group have the responsibility for reporting on or about their actions, they must work together. Referring questions to the group members is another strategy for giving recognition for quality involvement. Whether it is a question from a parent, the local newspaper, or the board of education, having it directed to one or more members of the group acknowledges that group members "know" about their work efforts and do not need a translator to inform others. It also is a strong indication of trust.

SUMMARY

Implementation will occur only through the work of the people in the organization. Principals must have skills and knowledge to facilitate this work of others. Whenever possible, principals must make implementation easier by:

- ◆ helping to clarify the tasks to be done
- ◆ providing resources for accomplishing the tasks
- ◆ making sure the appropriate people are involved in the planning and implementation of the tasks
- ◆ providing time for people to connect
- ◆ minimizing redundancies and overlaps in tasks
- ◆ creating completion timelines and "big picture maps" for viewing multiple projects simultaneously
- ◆ creating continuous feedback loops for evaluation and planning

To do this, principals need to develop and use skills in:

- listening
- questioning
- anticipating and predicting
- persistence and patience
- identifying and reducing resistance
- securing resources
- working with groups

Finally, principals need to foster the quality of involvement from others by using such strategies as:

- determining the level of involvement needed and desired
- modeling the involvement desired
- making use of the talents and expertise of organizational members
- making it easy to do
- recognizing and rewarding involvement

The information presented here should be considered a primer of what principals need to know and be able to do in facilitating the coordination and collaboration of tasks for successful implementation. Every opportunity should be taken to learn new strategies and fine-tune content and process skills.

FOLLOW-UP ACTIVITIES

1. Ask to attend meetings at other schools or units of the district. Do not try to become part of the meeting. What you want to do is practice your skills as a process observer and in identifying task and maintenance roles in the group. Let whomever you are observing know that your attendance is to help develop your own skills. However, if they are interested, offer to give feedback on what you observed. Be sure that initially all of your observations are with other groups rather than your own. Because you will be an "outsider" it will be much easier to observe objectively. Remember that your intent is to practice and become a skilled observer. The fewer distractions early on, the more time you can devote to skill development.

2. Identify individuals in your school who are interested in developing some of their own skills as facilitators. Set up a series of assigned role practice sessions. Have different individuals practice playing different task and maintenance roles; have one or more members serve as the process observer and deliver a report (both positive and negative) at the end of the observation.

3. Locate some "self-help" audio- and videotapes on developing listening skills. Use them as a part of your own professional development plan. Invite one or two colleagues to be your development observers; tell them what you are trying to learn about and become skilled in. Ask them to periodically give you feedback on your skill development and use.

4. Kick back, relax and watch a movie (or read a book). However, you are to select the movie (book) with a specific purpose in mind. You want to observe characters and situations in this movie (book) that operationalize implementation and/or exemplify one or more of the characteristics of leadership in implementation. There is a wide range of movies (books) from which to choose. You may have a favorite you'd like to see (read) again or a new one you've heard about; either is fine. Just remember to view (read) it with the purpose of looking for successful implementation and the characteristics of those in the story who help that occur. The following are some suggestions to get you started.

For examples of persistence, direction, and effort in implementing a project watch *The African Queen, Rudy, The Wizard of Oz,* or *Stand and Deliver.* For perspectives on providing resources, minimizing overlaps, and creating "big picture maps," watch *The Longest Day.* Take a look at *The Magnificent Seven, The Dirty Dozen,* or *Back to the Future* if you are interested in observing efforts to get the right people together. Anticipating and predicting are of paramount importance in *Apollo 13.*

5

MONITORING IMPLEMENTATION

At this point in the implementation process you know what it is you want to accomplish, you have identified the various tasks and secured the appropriate resources for doing it, and you have the people needed to accomplish it identified and trained. If you do not have these elements in place, what follows cannot help much excepting as it highlights the importance of planning before acting. There really is no reason to consider monitoring implementation if you don't know where you're headed, the general route you will take to get there, and the resources (human and nonhuman) you will need to make it happen. Simply put, you have nothing to monitor. The information that follows assumes your goals, plans, and resources have been readied. Each of these is essential for taking or initiating action. In this chapter, implementation is at the "Go" stage as in "Get Ready, Get Set, Go!" Put another way, it's "All aboard—the train is leaving the station!" Things are moving now.

To ensure that implementation continues to move rather than stall and to ensure that it moves in the planned direction, principals need specific knowledge and skills in monitoring implementation. In this chapter, the first priority is to understand why monitoring implementation is important. Next, what monitoring is, when and how it should be done, and some means for doing it are addressed. Then attention is given to using the information gathered to maintain, correct, or improve what is happening.

Finally, the chapter closes by citing guidelines to assist principals in setting up the necessary systems for monitoring progress and initiating corrective actions for achieving successful implementation.

WHY IS MONITORING IMPLEMENTATION IMPORTANT?

There are a variety of worthy responses to this question. A humorous response can be found in Murphy's Law. According to Murphy's Law (Martin, 1973), "If something can go wrong it will" and that "left to themselves, things always go from bad to worse." Monitoring implementation is a means for assuring that things aren't "left to themselves" and that things don't "go from bad to worse." When principals and other school leaders are monitoring, Murphy's prognostications can be avoided.

On the more serious side, DuFour and Eaker (1992) use "paying attention" as a synonym for monitoring. They admonish principals to "...monitor all aspects of a school's programs" because monitoring (paying attention) is "a key vehicle for communicating the values of the school" (p. 97). Similarly, Schein (cited in Yukl, 1989) noted that "Leaders communicate their priorities, values, and concerns by their choice of things to ask about, measure, comment on, praise, and criticize. Much of this communication occurs during monitoring and planning activities..." (p. 213).

Additional evidence of why monitoring is important can be found in the NPBEA Knowledge and Skills Base document. In "Section 6: Implementation," "monitor progress" is presented as one of five facets of an implementation process model. It is asserted that monitoring progress enables principals "...to assess whether the implementation process is on schedule and whether it is running smoothly and staying within resource estimates" (p. 6-5). Additionally, monitoring progress precedes the facet of the model labeled "Reassess." Under the heading "Reassessment and Modification," the NPBEA declares that "Effective principals use monitoring and evaluation information to make decisions about the plans or action steps they should continue and/or revise" (p. 6-9)

Based on the model presented by NPBEA, if "monitor progress" is bypassed or neglected, a gap is created between "Set Plan In Motion" and "Reassess." The gap results in a cycle of "do and change—do and change—do and change...." Unfortunately, the reasons for what is done and why changes are made are missing. This, in turn, creates a situation in which "anything done would be as good as any other thing done since it all will be changed for no reason anyway."

Sadly, the "do and change" cycle is alive and well in many schools today. Staff members often refer to the "do and change" cycle as "TYNT" (This Year's New Thing); they have come to realize that it is wise not to invest too much time in any one thing for soon it will be changed to something else. Additionally, they know that no one will use monitoring and evaluation information for making any of these decisions to change. Monitoring is essential if we are to modify the "do and change" cycle to include changes based on information for improved performance rather than change for change's sake.

Leading authors representing education, business, and industry have had much to say about the importance of monitoring. The following citations are offered in support of the proposition that monitoring is absolutely essential to successful implementation.

- *Taking Charge of Change* (1987, p. 77) by Shirley Hord, William Rutherford, Leslie Huling-Austin, and Gene Hall:

  The effective CFs [Change Facilitators] we observed in our studies sought objective data to help them assess progress in implementing their new programs. They gathered information about what was happening with an innovation and about the status and progress of teachers as they were introduced to, started working with, and become experienced in using new school practices. Though the importance of monitoring activities is gaining increased recognition, particularly through recent research on effective principals (Rutherford, 1985), this category of intervention is often neglected.... [M]onitoring must take place to ensure a successful improvement effort.

- *Leadership Secrets of Attila the Hun* (1987, p. 63) by Wess Roberts:

  The following are among the "responsibilities of a chieftain" which Attila shared with his followers and the chieftains of other tribes:

"Chieftains must teach their Huns well that which is expected of them. Otherwise, Huns will probably do something not expected of them."

"Chieftains must inspect their Huns frequently in order to see that what is accomplished meets with what is expected."

♦ *What's worth fighting for?: Working together for your school* (1991, p. 83) by Michael Fullan and Andy Hargreaves:

In effective schools, teachers working with other teachers and the administration are preoccupied with "measuring what is important" (Peters, 1987). Simple, direct, meaningful, involved forms of monitoring become natural, regular concerns of all teachers.

♦ *Checklist for Change* (1990, pp. 84–85) by Thomas Harvey:

Nothing works for long on automatic pilot, not even a plane or a boat. Similarly, change plans will falter unless there is a system for monitoring implementation of action plans and their effectiveness in reaching the desired point B. In the arcane language of evaluation, you need to carry out formative, process, and output discrepancy analysis.... [S]uffice it to say that if you never check on your progress, you'll never know when you've arrived.

♦ *The Challenge of Organizational Change* (1992, p. 513) by Rosabeth Moss Kanter, Barry Stein, and Todd Jick:

How do we know the change has happened? How do we know if it has been successful? Along the way, how do we know it's on track and that events are likely to lead to the desired change? How can we get information to monitor the impact of the process of the change on the people carrying it out?...Routine data collection...can allow the change management team to monitor progress and make midcourse adjustments.

♦ *The Restructuring Handbook: A Guide to School Revitalization* (1994, pp. 138–39) by Kathryn Whitaker and Monte Moses:

...[E]ducators tend to dismiss close monitoring of performance and progress under a variety of rationalizations....[T]he failure to closely scrutinize current performance cripples efforts to improve because there is no defined starting place....Quality improvement is not something that happens by reviewing results once a year with one standardized test score. It is a day-by-day and moment-by-moment affair.

♦ "Demonstrating the benefits of staff development: An interview with Thomas R. Guskey" (1994, p. 64) by Guy Todnem and Michael Warner in *The Journal of Staff Development*:

...[W]e must recognize that evaluation information not only serves a summative purpose to determine whether or not something works, but it also serves an extremely important formative purpose....[W]e need to be constantly checking what's working and where there are difficulties....[W]e need to be ready to intervene so that those difficulties do not become major problems.

♦ "Highlights from research of effective school leadership" (1982, p. 349) by ASCD's Research Information Service in *Educational Leadership*:

Effective schools have effective leaders....[T]here are six leadership behaviors that have been consistently associated with schools that are well managed and whose students achieve....They monitor student achievement on a regular basis. Principals set expectations for the entire school and check to make sure those expectations are being met. They know how well their students are performing as compared to students in other schools.

♦ "Key ingredients for successful implementation of just-in-time: A system for all business sizes" (1994, p. 64) by Marvin Tucker and David Davis in *Business Horizons:*

As with any program, operating procedures must be monitored. Results of the changes made must be reviewed. Most likely, areas that need fine-tuning will be discovered....Peak system performance is maintained only when monitoring and reviewing procedures and policies are in place and enforced.

Taken individually, each quote reports on the importance of some aspect of monitoring. Taken as a group, themes that focus on why monitoring implementation is important begin to appear:

♦ Monitoring provides information about what is happening and if what is happening fits with expectations

♦ Monitoring occurs in all programs, processes, or projects, and in all facets of each program, process, or project

♦ Monitoring involves individuals at all levels of the organization

♦ Monitoring keeps the program, process, or project from faltering and/or failing

♦ Monitoring is essential for ensuring quality and a successful improvement effort

♦ Monitoring provides the information that reports on progress and informs proposed adjustments (changes)

♦ Monitoring helps to communicate what is important in the organization

♦ Monitoring helps us know where we started, how far we have come, and how much farther we have to go

♦ Monitoring allows information regarding performance to be provided frequently and regularly

♦ Monitoring helps prevent problems

Just these few passages and the messages they offer, along
with the earlier references to Murphy, DuFour and Eaker, and
NPBEA's Model, should help principals understand that monitoring is vital to successful implementation.

The purpose of monitoring is to ensure plans become realities. Questions such as, "Are we on schedule?," "Are we within budget?," "Are we using all of the materials we allocated for
this work?," "Are the individuals within the groups working
well?," "Are students using longer sentences?," "Are they
reading more?," "Can they accurately solve complex problems
more often?," "Are staff members planning together?," and
numerous others must be asked and answered. Once we have
the information to respond to these and other questions, we
evaluate and make judgments about what should be done
next. In other words, monitoring provides the information
upon which decisions for actions are made, which in turn
keeps implementation on track. It is important to remember
that if implementation is not "on track," then things must be
"off track." Monitoring to improve (formative) and monitoring to judge (summative) informs a variety of decisions that
need to be made if successful implementation is to be achieved. Implementation efforts that fail to incorporate effective
monitoring will most likely fail and, once again, students,
teachers, and parents lose.

WHAT IS MONITORING?

Defining monitoring involves blending information about
why monitoring is important and identifying its critical components. DuFour and Eaker (1992) offered "paying attention"
as a synonym for monitoring. According to Harvey (1990), "In
the arcane language of evaluation, you need to carry out formative, process, and output discrepancy analysis" (p. 84). In line
with this, the following statement appears under the heading
of "Monitor Progress" in the NPBEA's *Principals for Our Changing Schools* (6-9): "Effective principals systematically gather information on a project's progress: what has been accomplished;
what obstacles must be overcome; whether action steps are on

schedule; whether resources are being used more, or less, quickly than anticipated, etc." Likewise, McLaughlin (1990), Popham (1990), and Tuckman (1985) stress the importance of gathering information that informs regarding progress and, when necessary, is useful in determining appropriate corrective actions.

Given the above, it seems reasonable for our purposes to define monitoring as:

> focusing on a project, process or program by gathering information that (a) indicates whether or not expectations are being achieved, and (b) if not, provides relevant data for designing needed adjustments or corrective actions, which will result in achievement of expectations.

Because the intended results of initiated projects, programs and/or processes are improvements, monitoring implementation involves two critical areas—gathering information about what is going on and initiating corrective actions as needed. Without the gathering of information the response to "How are we doing?" is, at best, a guess. Suggested changes in actions without a base of information for making them end up being "change for change's sake." It is the combining of the two that allows for improvement.

The overall framework for monitoring should be developed at the planning stages of the program, process, or project. This early consideration assures that monitoring is part of the plan, not an afterthought, and reinforces that monitoring is not an event, but a continuous process which must be led and managed over the life of the program, project, or process being implemented. Establishing a monitoring system at the planning phase helps create a context for successful implementation by:

♦ Identifying periodic checkpoints for monitoring

This helps make monitoring a part of the routine activities of the implementation. All monitoring activities are assigned due dates and are given as responsibilities to someone on the project team in the written plan.

♦ Securing resource allocations of money, time and personnel to carry out this work

Because lack of funds, lack of time, and no one available to conduct the work are among the reasons frequently given as to why evaluations are not done, funds, time, and personnel need to be included in the initial plans.

♦ Defining who will monitor, what will be monitored, when monitoring activities will be done, and what means will be used to collect information

After the project, program, or process is underway is a poor time to be making decisions about what data to collect, what instruments to use, when to gather information, and so forth; this is too late. These decisions need to be made and the specifics included in the planning documents.

♦ Connecting it to the other elements of the plan

"System" implies an interconnectedness to other parts of the project, program, or process being implemented. In a system, activities in any one part of the system affect activities in every other part of the system. This is true for monitoring.

A context for successful implementation requires a comprehensive monitoring system. Some of the knowledge and skills principals will need for creating such a context are discussed in the following sections: when and how monitoring should be done; gathering information; and the use of feedback. Additionally, some frameworks for aligning monitoring tasks with other elements of implementation are offered.

WHEN AND HOW SHOULD MONITORING BE DONE?

The basic answer to the "when" part of this question is:

whenever it is important to know if the expectations of a project, process, or program are being achieved so that either current efforts can be maintained or corrective actions can be initiated.

Because myriad projects, processes, and programs are happening all at once in a school, monitoring should be done continually, and it should allow for different efforts to be monitored differentially. And so, the response to the "how" part of this question is:

> in a variety of ways that fit differing situations yet provide the information needed to determine if expectations are being achieved so that either current efforts can be maintained or corrective actions can be initiated.

A monitoring system structured around the types of implementation found in schools—routine (daily and periodic), new or nonroutine, and unique (discussed in Chapter 2)—coupled with three general approaches for monitoring—scanning, focused, and probing—that allow for variations in intensity and frequency levels, can guide both the "when" and "how" of monitoring almost any project, process, or program. The information gathered through these approaches provides a basis for adjustment and/or maintenance decisions, as well as how best to continue monitoring most effectively. Different types of implementation require different frequencies and intensity levels of monitoring activities.

SCANNING: MONITORING ROUTINE IMPLEMENTATION

Recall that routine implementation activities are those that have become predictable and generally automatic. Activities such as opening each school day, cleaning of the building, taking attendance, creating a master schedule, and making student classroom assignments can all be categorized as routine. It is very important, however, to understand that even though these activities are routine, they need to be monitored. In fact, it is a credit to the monitoring system that these activities continue working routinely. Information regarding the achievement of the expectations for routine projects, processes, and programs are gathered continually.

The approach most likely to be appropriate for monitoring routine implementation is *scanning*. Scanning involves continuously surveying to assure that everything is operating as expected. Scanning uses techniques that are unobtrusive and constant, unless something out of the ordinary is spotted. Like routine implementation, scanning operates at a level of automaticity. The *American Heritage Dictionary* (1982) defines scanning as " to look over quickly but thoroughly by moving from one point to another" (p. 1095). Scanning is the level of monitoring that teachers employ once their classroom management procedures are in place. The teacher looks about the classroom and listens. If everyone and everything is operating as expected, the teacher returns attention to the current task. If something is determined as not acceptable according to expectations, then the attention of the teacher is focused on the area or individual of concern.

Scanning is the kind of monitoring that principals do as they enter the building each day. They scan the walls, the doors, the hallways, the parking lots, and myriad other places and things that support the implementation of a smooth school day. Their eyes and ears take in the areas quickly. They are looking and listening for things "as usual." Only when something is not as expected does a conscious registering occur. If something unusual is picked up, the scanning is interrupted and a different level (a deeper level) of monitoring is initiated.

Scanning can be used to monitor such things as the physical elements of the school, varied aspects of student behavior, use of classroom space and time, and teaching methods being employed. If the information gathered via the scanning signals trouble or disruption in the routine, a greater level of intensity will need to be initiated to determine what has caused the disruption and what needs to be done to restore routine. Based on the information gathered, current behaviors, resource allocations, and other components are continued, abandoned, or adjusted as needed until the expectations are restored.

FOCUSED: MONITORING SOMETHING NEW OR DIFFERENT

The second type of implementation reviewed in Chapter 2 was "new or nonroutine." New or nonroutine implementation generally involves the start and successful continuation of new programs and procedures. Activities such as using a new textbook, learning new methods for teaching reading, establishing a peer coaching program for staff, or developing discipline procedures to align with new legislation are all examples of new or nonroutine implementation efforts. Establishing something new requires not only that monitoring be done continually, but that it be done with greater intensity and frequency.

Additionally, it requires concentration in a few areas rather than moving quickly over many areas; that is, it is *focused*.

Focused monitoring requires more concentration and narrows the number of things on which information is gathered. This is especially true as the various components of the new projects, processes, or programs are just getting started. Newness creates feelings of unfamiliarity and awkwardness, and therefore requires monitoring (paying attention) more often and with greater concentration until the new behaviors begin to take on some routine qualities. As the first components of a new project, process, or program become more established (i.e., move toward routine), the intensity and frequency of the monitoring may be decreased on these early aspect(s) and refocused on the next component(s) of the effort. Once some aspects of the new effort have become routinized, scanning can be used to monitor them, while focused monitoring is used on the newly initiated components of the effort.

Focused monitoring should also be used when scanning identifies a disruption or problem in an established routine. As noted earlier, scanning moves quickly but thoroughly from one point to another as long as things are operating as expected. However, when a problem is identified, a closer, more detailed look at the problem point(s) needs to be initiated. For example, if in moving through the building the principal's scanning picks up an unusual amount of noise and movement in a particular area of the building, focused monitoring should be used. The principal should move to that area and gather more information about what is happening and why. Or, suppose the principal is scanning various reports on student achievement and comes across data that don't align with the other information on the reports. The principal's approach for monitoring should switch from scanning to focused. Attention should be concentrated on this apparent discrepancy.

Trying to locate what might account for the disruption or problem is what focused monitoring is intended to do. Whether it is unusual noise and movement in the building or a discrepancy between expected and reported student performance data, an explanation is sought through focused monitoring. Focused monitoring might reveal that there is a special activity underway that demands movement and conversation, or that the class is not staffed as scheduled, or that a student or staff member has become ill or had an accident. Each of these can be aligned with expectations through resource allocation or behavior adjustments and the routine restored. Regarding the discrepancy on the student performance information, focused monitoring might reveal a printing or arithmetic error in reporting, or an incomplete report due to student illness, or that an individual performance report was given where a group report should have been. Again, with the explanations discovered, the necessary adjustments can be made.

It is possible, however, that the information gathered through focused monitoring does not provide what is necessary to explain why the problem or disruption is occurring. When this is the case, an approach for monitoring which provides even more intensity and frequency is needed; that is, *probing* is required.

PROBING: FINDING OUT WHY

Probing requires that the search for causes go deeper and take on an exploratory, even investigative, purpose. Probes go beyond the surface; they require generating new data and/or reviewing data in the disaggregate. Probing may require detailed analysis of individual parts of a situation, as well as the context in which the situation is occurring. Probing is an approach to find out why something is or is not happening; it may require looking in areas that initially do not seem to be related to the identified problem, yet affect it through various connections in the system. If focused monitoring does not reveal the cause of a problem or disruption so it can be corrected, then probing should be used to accumulate additional information from a variety of sources until the why of a situation is revealed.

One example in which probing revealed a cause of discrepancies in student performance data occurred at a large comprehensive high school. The discrepancy was an unusually large percentage of students reported as failing a required history course. Probing revealed that the failing students were in different sections of the course, but all of them had the same instructor. Additionally, student performance reports from those class sections earlier in the year revealed only a few students were failing the course. Similar reports from previous years indicated the same pattern of a few failing students early, with a large percentage of failing students at about the same point in the school year in the history section taught by this instructor. Conversations with the instructor and students revealed a cause for the failures that neither scanning nor focused monitoring would have discovered. That is, each year at this particular time students were to bring in specific materials for an assigned project. Students were told that if they did not bring the materials, they would receive an F for the grading period. Large numbers of students either did not or could not bring the materials as assigned and therefore were assigned an F for the grading period. Probing revealed that the student performance report was really about materials not history concepts. The reallocation of a few dollars in supply funds provided for purchase of the required materials and allowed both teacher and student to refocus on teaching and learning history concepts.

Probing can be helpful with the implementation of new or nonroutine efforts and with problems or disruptions in routine implementation efforts. As causes of problems are revealed and adjustments are initiated to solve them, monitoring can move back into a focused approach. Maintaining focused monitoring for a period of time allows the opportunity to see if the actions taken move the achieved results back in line with the expected results. When focused monitoring has provided evidence of the return to aligned expectations and achievements, then scanning can be instituted again as the approach for monitoring the situation.

AS NEEDED: MONITORING UNIQUE SITUATIONS

The third type of implementation deals with unique activities. These happen less frequently, are often less localized in initiation, and regularly involve individuals from many levels of the organization and some from outside education. The actions needed to successfully implement unique activities must be clear, practiced periodically, and communicated to those who will be involved in the implementation. Resources for successfully implementing unique activities must be available constantly.

Unique types of implementation include arranging for a visiting dignitary, a security crisis, weather emergencies, construction of a new facility, and other similar activities.

The levels of intensity and the frequency of monitoring activities for unique implementation are generally extremely high. Unique situations are often short in duration but require plenty of attention to multiple components simultaneously. Approaches for monitoring unique implementation situations need to accommodate the required intensity and frequency levels. It is likely to be the case that all three of the monitoring approaches will be used during unique implementation situations.

ALWAYS PAYING ATTENTION: WHENEVER AND WHATEVER IT TAKES

Principals are reminded that during any school year, the vast majority of the implementation will be of a routine type (daily and/or periodic). Certainly, each year will bring some new implementation efforts and perhaps even a unique type. But something is always being monitored and one or more of the approaches described here (scanning, focused, and probing) will be in use constantly.

Basically, then, the "when" of monitoring is continual and the "how" depends on the situation. Continuous monitoring activities for routine projects, processes, and programs need to be built into a system. Additionally, plans to provide resources necessary for identified adjustments in routine implementation activities must be included. A determination of what new implementation efforts will be undertaken during a specific year must be made. If too many efforts in any one year are new type implementation, problems are likely to occur. Part of these problems result from an inability to monitor things at the levels of intensity and frequency that are needed to get them established.

Finally, as is true with so many things in life, you just have to plan for the unexpected. Some unique implementation activities are known ahead of time, but others occur unannounced and they must be monitored—like it or not! Simply put, principals must do all they can to ensure that *all* school operations are appropriately monitored.

WHAT MEANS EXIST FOR MONITORING IMPLEMENTATION?

In addition to making quality decisions about when to monitor, principals need to determine the means to be used in monitoring.

According to the *American Heritage Dictionary* (1982), a means is a "method, course of action, or instrument by which an act can be accomplished or some end achieved." This definition reminds us of the significant function served by implementation's goals and objectives: they provide a context for determining the means for monitoring. The goals and objectives of the program, process, or project being implemented should be the driving force in determining the means for monitoring. While it sounds obvious, there are many instances when the means used to monitor have little or no relevance to the project, program, or process being implemented. Therefore, the first step principals should take in identifying the means for monitoring is to put the written goals and objectives of the project, program, or process in a prominent place. With the written goals and objectives available for easy reference the principal and other members of a project team can use them as criteria for evaluating the appropriateness of suggested means for monitoring.

For example, if the program objective is to improve math achievement of students in grades 6, 7, and 8, then the means for monitoring the implementation should relate directly to this. What would help principals know whether math achievement in grades 6, 7, and 8 is improving? Possible means for monitoring this program might include measures of student and teacher attitudes toward math; student scores on the math sections of the standardized achievement tests; teacher records regarding students' performance on daily assignments and tests; attendance records; teacher feedback regarding the usefulness of the math textbook; and student grades in math. Which of these means should be used? While a case might be made for each of them, some are more directly related than others. Given the objective of improving student achievement in math, initial monitoring would focus on relevant standardized test data and teacher records regarding student performance.

Consider the goal of reducing the amount of teacher talk and increasing the amount of student talk in classroom interactions. What means could be used to monitor the achievement of this goal? The means could include interviews with students; interviews with teachers; classroom observations; student and teacher surveys regarding classroom interactions; video- or audiotaping of class sessions; student attendance in various classes; information regarding the teaching materials used; student grades; and parent surveys. Again, some of these means are more directly related to the goals than others. Monitoring implementation of this effort suggests the use of classroom observations, student interviews, and video- or audiotapings. While all of the means listed may provide useful information, those suggested are more directly related to the goals and objectives of the effort.

Direct relationship to the goals and objectives of the program, project, or process being implemented is the primary criterion for determining which means should be used in monitoring. Once the means are determined to be directly related to the goals and objectives, two additional criteria can be applied. First, the means to be used should be affordable. Affordable refers not only to monetary cost, but also time, human resources, and equipment needs. If the resource demands of a proposed means exceeds those available, it is inappropriate. Second, the means must be usable. If the information gathered is directly related to the goal, but those who need the information can't understand it or make use of it to improve implementation, then the it is not appropriate. Examples of this are sophisticated statistics, or charts and graphs without identifying information, or page after page of observation notes with no explanation or context for interpretation. While such means may be directly related to the goals and objectives, they are inappropriate because they cannot be used.

Principals should use three criteria for determining the appropriateness of a means for monitoring implementation:

- Is it directly related to the goals and objectives of the program, project, or process being implemented?
- Is it affordable?
- Does it provide information that can be used?

If responses to these three questions are positive then the mean under consideration should be used for monitoring implementation. Situations vary and require that principals and their project teams use discretion in applying the three criteria to fit particular needs. However, it is certainly the case that the criteria relationship to the goals and objectives of the implementation effort is the least flexible. The three questions should be asked and answered in the order presented here. Low costs and utility of presentation are of no value if the means are not directly related to intent of the effort!

Once the means for monitoring implementation have been determined as appropriate by the process described, then locating or generating the relevant information becomes the task. A great deal of information useful in monitoring implementation is already available in schools. Pankake and Burnett (1990) pointed out that information of all kinds is collected daily, weekly, monthly, and annually. For example, data such as student attendance, immunization records, standardized test scores, end-of-semester grades, staff attendance, and equipment and supply purchases are collected regularly in most schools. The information may be collected for reasons other than monitoring the implementation of a program, project, or process in the school. Still, if the information is determined to be directly related to the goals and objectives of the effort, it should be used for the purpose of monitoring as well.

Likewise, activities of all sorts are constantly underway in schools. Some of these activities are formally planned and others occur incidentally. Students, teachers, support staff, administrators, and others are selecting things to do that are intended to result in specific accomplishments. Many of these activities may be important for monitoring the implementation of a particular program, project, or process. The application of the three-step process for identifying means for monitoring may indicate that these existing activities have direct relationships to the goals and objectives of the implementation effort. If so, the information generated needs to be accessed and applied as means for monitoring. For example, teachers keep behavior records on one or more students in a class. They generally record lesson plans and display charts of classroom achievements for specific academic areas—spelling, multiplication facts, student stories, and so forth—Students write in individual journals, records regarding homework assignments are entered in grade books, and various facilities are scheduled for projects (library, art rooms, gymnasium, cafeteria). Use these existing data when they are relevant.

Using the earlier example of improving math performance of students in grades 6, 7, and 8, existing information such as standardized test scores, end-of-semester grades, charts of classroom achievements, and records about homework appear to be information sources directly related to monitoring. Similarly, the example of monitoring increases in student talk and decreases in teacher talk in classroom interactions might benefit from using existing information sources such as student journals and teacher lesson plans. Not all information needed for monitoring implementation will already be in existence in the school; however, starting with an examination of what information is already in place is a smart use of time, energy, and resources. If data for monitoring have been identified as important to determining the progress toward or achievement of the goals and objectives of implementation but do not already exist, then they must be generated.

Generating new databases can be expensive and labor intensive. Given that money, time, and energy are limited resources, only data that are affordable and usable should be collected. Finally, principals could do much to improve the means dimension of monitoring the schools' operations by creating an in-house quality assurance group representing all faculty and staff personnel. Its mission would be to ensure the adequate and appropriate monitoring of designated programs and projects. Such action could dramatically improve the efficiency and effectiveness of the school's implementation efforts.

USING THE INFORMATION FROM MONITORING TO MAINTAIN, CORRECT, OR IMPROVE WHAT IS HAPPENING

According to Hunter (1982), "To practice without knowledge of results is usually a waste of time" (p. 68). As individuals and groups engage in the activities they have identified as important for implementing a particular program or process, they need to receive feedback regarding progress toward the desired results. Feedback helps differentiate between efforts and accomplishments, between assuming and knowing, and between busyness and productivity. Feedback is essential in ensuring the progress of implementation; it should be frequent and provided at critical decision points. Additionally, specific information on what actions might be taken to improve performance is also important. Guskey (1985; 1995) calls this kind of information "corrective." He emphasizes that not only do we need to know "how we are doing," we also need to know how we can improve our performance. For Guskey, feedback *with* correctives is the key to improved performance. While both Hunter and Guskey were writing with specific reference to students, they are describing the two points critical to monitoring implementation at any level.

Popham (1990) illustrates how feedback can be useful to teachers by describing "en route" or enabling skills tests. The items on the test measure the enabling skills required for mastery of the terminal skill. He notes, "Such tests, when administered to students who have completed instruction judged to be ineffectual, will usually help teachers identify the en route skills that students have failed to master. In revising the instruction, therefore, the teacher now has access to some cues regarding the improvement of the instructional sequence, namely, to emphasize more strongly or explain more lucidly the content associated with the en route skills that are troubling students" (pp. 387-88).

In the example of the improvement of math performance for students in grades 6, 7, and 8, students will not only need opportunity to practice the math concepts introduced to them through instruction, they will also need information regarding the kinds of error they are making and how to correct those errors. Students need to be informed of their performance. For example, "your answers to 6 of the 10 problems were correct." That is certainly better than just doing the problems and never knowing what the results were. However, even more powerful would be: "Your answers to 6 of the 10 problems were correct. On the ones that were incorrect, you failed to add the subtotals before multiplying. If you will do your addition of subtotals before you multiply, you will probably calculate all of the problems correctly on the next assignment." Now the student knows not only the results of his efforts, but also how his behavior can be changed to improve his performance.

Similarly, the teacher or teachers working to improve math performance of students in grades 6, 7, and 8 also need feedback and correctives regarding their efforts to implement. They need information not only on how their students performed on math tests, but also what errors the students made. If the kinds of error that students made are similar, then teachers can re-teach the concepts in that area. If errors are from a variety of sources and appear to be generated from carelessness, emphasis on checking work and careful calculations can be planned. Feedback might provide teachers with the information that students performed well on calculation items but did poorly on items that required reading through information to locate the information needed for calculation. Continuing current efforts in practice calculations would be appropriate, but the feedback regarding reading would need to be processed so that ideas for correcting and improving student strategies for performing in this area could be developed.

An important purpose for monitoring implementation is to provide feedback. The feedback is then to be used to generate actions that either maintain, correct, or improve the results of the program, process, or project being implemented. If information is gathered but not used to make necessary adjustments in the implementation efforts, it is data collection, but it is not monitoring. For data collection to contribute to monitoring implementation:

♦ knowledge of results is needed
♦ a system for feeding this knowledge back to those responsible for implementation must be developed
♦ indications of what adjustments are needed to align results with expectations must be provided to those responsible for implementation
♦ needed adjustments must be implemented that maintain, correct, or improve results

GUIDELINES FOR MONITORING PROGRESS AND INITIATING CORRECTIVE ACTION FOR SUCCESSFUL IMPLEMENTATION

Based on the information in this chapter, nine guidelines for actions that principals and other school leaders can take in monitoring the process of implementation and initiating corrective actions are presented. These guidelines are not the only actions that can or should be taken in performing these important tasks. Additionally, they are guidelines not rules. Thus, principals are reminded to use their own good judgment in determining what might be the best actions for their particular situations. No set of guidelines can substitute for knowledgeable and skilled leadership.

♦ Make monitoring a part of the implementation process

Monitoring is embedded in the process of implementation, not parallel to it. The monitoring system must be established early and used continuously. It should not be an afterthought to the activities, but rather a part of the implementation process itself. Monitoring should occur along the way rather than as an event at the end of the effort, or worse, not at all. Monitoring must be embedded in the process. To remove it or to neglect it is to ignore a vital part of successful implementation.

Monitoring implementation is not an event but something that must be led and managed over the life of the implementation project. It must inform regarding whether expectations are being met and, if not, what revisions are in order.

♦ Make sure each person understands that monitoring is his or her responsibility

Everyone in the school has some responsibility for monitoring implementation. Students have the responsibility of monitoring their behaviors and the quality of their work. Teachers, among other things, monitor activities in their classrooms, check for student understanding of instruction, work at putting into practice new behaviors and teaching methods, and talk with their colleagues about successes and problems they are experiencing. Principals are responsible for monitoring activities such as gathering information, feeding information back to those responsible for implementation, setting periodic points for progress checks, and providing resources for gathering, organizing, and disseminating data regarding results and expectations. Anyone associated with the school has responsibilities for assuring that what is supposed to happen actually happens.

♦ Realize that if monitoring isn't done, the initiative is likely to fail.

Because monitoring is synonymous with "paying attention," when monitoring isn't being done it means no one is paying attention. We all know what happens in life generally when no one is paying attention—wrecks, spills, overgrown gardens, illnesses, accidents, and other disagreeable and disastrous consequences result. It is the same with program, process, and project initiatives in schools: anything that isn't being monitored is in jeopardy. Whether it is the safety of children on the playground, the involvement of staff in decisions, the achievement of students in math, or the development of reading skills in young children, someone needs to be paying attention to see that expectations are being realized. Remember Murphy's warnings: "If something can go wrong, it will" and "left to themselves, things always go from bad to worse."

♦ Build monitoring into the initial plan

Monitoring is a necessary part of the implementation process, not an add-on. Yet, monitoring is often the most neglected and least attended to element of implementation. One way to combat this tendency toward neglect is to make regular use of the project plans developed at the initiation stages of implementation efforts. In those plans, the who, what, and when of implementation is specifically outlined. Use these documents as guides to determine periodic check points to verify that what was planned has been done. The information that is gathered at these periodic checkpoints can then be fed back into the system and necessary adjustments can be made.

♦ Monitor everything

If there is something being implemented, that is, being made to happen, in your school that isn't being monitored, trouble is brewing. If it is supposed to happen but isn't being monitored, it is in jeopardy of failing. On the other hand, if it isn't supposed to occur but is, you will soon have a different sort of problem in trying to explain that this occurred because you weren't paying attention! In either of these situations, the problems can be avoided by monitoring everything. Monitoring everything is the way to be sure that what is supposed to happen in your school does and that what isn't supposed to happen doesn't.

♦ Adjust the type of monitoring to fit the situation

While everything needs to monitored, everything does not need the same kind of monitoring. Variations in the frequency and intensity of monitoring activities should be done to fit the situation. Not unlike the saying about swallowing the camel and choking on the gnat, you don't want to use probing techniques in a situation that needs scanning. On the other hand, continuing to monitor through scanning makes little sense if expectations and results don't match even after adjustments are implemented. This would be as productive as the arranging of deck chairs on the Titanic. Probing to discover what is happening and why is essential in such a situation. Principals must be able to assess various situations and determine the best monitoring behaviors to use in each.

♦ Use the goals and objectives of the programs, processes, and projects to drive the monitoring system

What to monitor, when, and how to do it can all best be identified by using the goals and objectives of the program, process, or project being monitored. Information collected and used for decision-making should be directly related to the goals and objectives of the implementation effort. While other criteria for selecting means for monitoring were also presented, the mean's relatedness to the goals and objectives must be given first priority.

♦ Keep everyone informed of the information gathered

This can assist in keeping efforts focused. Disseminating written information on a topic draws attention to it; requesting individuals to report information on a topic, draws attention to it; placing a topic on a meeting agenda draws attention to it; and scheduling a conference to discuss a particular topic draws attention to it. Keeping people informed is a way of focusing their attention. If monitoring really does mean "paying attention," it makes sense that keeping everyone informed is a powerful way for keeping everyone paying attention, that is, monitoring.

◆ Remember that the reason to monitor is to ensure effectiveness

If monitoring isn't producing useful information to maintain, correct, or improve implementation, then something is wrong. Monitoring should provide both knowledge of results and guides for corrective action. Knowledge without action is neglect; the reverse is a careless use of limited resources.

SUMMARY

Given the important enabling relationship that monitoring has to successful implementation, it is difficult to understand why this task often receives less than adequate attention. Principals must acquire and use monitoring knowledge and skills if they expect to be leaders of successful implementation. Reasons given for less than optimal monitoring of implementation include lack of time, lack of money, specific criteria are not available for measuring, inability to identify measurable objectives, and no helpful tools available.

This chapter addressed these reasons and dismissed them as "excuses" for neglecting to monitor implementation. As Du-Four and Eaker (1992) noted, principals need to monitor all aspects of their schools. If, as they assert, monitoring is paying attention, then principals will pay attention to what they believe to be important; that is, they will monitor it. Rarely do school leaders announce that this or that program is really not important, or that this or that activity is more important than another. Soon teachers, students, parents, and others realize what's important and what is not important by noting the monitoring levels used with any program, project, or process. What the principal "pays attention" to communicates effectively. If principals want programs, projects, or processes to be implemented effectively, they need to set the cadence and content for monitoring activities and results.

FOLLOW-UP ACTIVITIES

1. Invite a colleague, administrative intern/student, or staff member to "shadow" you for two or three days. Ask this person to observe your monitoring behaviors and categorize them as scanning, focusing, or probing. Have the observer record your behaviors on a matrix:

- down the left-hand side of the matrix list the type of activity: routine, new/nonroutine, and unique
- across the top of the matrix list monitoring categories: scanning, focused, probing
- ask the person shadowing you to identify your activities as routine, new/nonroutine, or unique
- also ask the person to check-off the monitoring category for each activity

At the end of the shadowing period, review the matrices to determine if there appears to be a pattern of both the types of activities (routine, new/nonroutine, or unique) and the monitoring categories you use (scanning, focused, or probing). Are you pleased with what these data reveal about your monitoring behaviors? Should you make any changes based on this information?

2. Pull out copies of any school improvement plans for your organization. Use the four points for establishing a monitoring system to evaluate the quality of the monitoring system described in the improvement plans.

If you are pleased with the monitoring system you have established for these plans, give yourself and your team a pat on the back. If you are not pleased with the system established, or find that no system has been established, then call the team together and use these four points to create a quality monitoring system for your plans—then use it!

3. Inventory the various data sources available in your school (building, classroom, and subject levels). Have all staff participate in identifying these sources. Once sources are identified, use webbing or mindmapping to begin connecting the data to projects, programs, or processes that might be used to monitor them. A good source for an overview of webbing and mindmapping is ASCD's *Visual Tools for Constructing Knowledge* by David Hyerle (1996).

6

SUPPORTING THOSE RESPONSIBLE FOR IMPLEMENTATION

One of the seven elements identified earlier (Chapter 3) as important in creating a context for implementation was the securing of long-term support. The point was made that a common occurrence with implementation of programs is the reduction of needed support once the effort is underway, which is almost certain to derail the program. Providing support early and maintaining it throughout the implementation process are critical responsibilities for principals. If comprehensive support is not present at start, there is little reason to expect it will be later. It must be established early, consistently, and from a variety of sources both internal and external to the school. While the momentum of enthusiasm can sustain some actions at the beginning of a project, it is not sufficient commitment as implementation proceeds. The focus of this chapter is on the knowledge and skills principals can use in creating a climate of support for those responsible for implementation.

Support means different things to different people. Like "beauty," it is in the eyes of the beholder. Therefore, principals must be aware of the wide range of things perceived as support by different individuals. For some people, support can mean resources such as materials, money, and personnel. For others, knowledge in the form of training and development activities may be a high priority. Providing time and/or attention can also be viewed as support. Additionally, it is important to remember that things perceived as support at one point in the implementation effort may not be perceived as such later on. As Fullan (1991) pointed out, "…precise needs are often not clear at the beginning, especially with complex changes. People often become clearer about their needs only when they start doing things, that is, during implementation itself" (p. 69). And so, there are likely to be as many different perceptions of support as there are individuals and groups involved in the implementation effort. Still, principals are expected to know what's needed, when, and by whom.

The more knowledge and skills principals can acquire related to identifying, providing, and assessing the support needed for implementation, the better. Knowledge about effective staff development, organizational context and culture, generation of resources, accountability, and motivation assists principals in supporting those responsible for implementation. Skills in delegating, restructuring the organization, changing the organizational culture, communicating openly, and nurturing professional growth in self and others are used repeatedly by principals in their efforts to provide support.

For example, if some form of block scheduling is planned for implementation at the school, the principal will need to apply knowledge and skills from a variety of areas in supporting those who must make this happen. Staff development regarding the what, why, and how of block scheduling will likely be important early on. However, as things get underway, additional development activities to help individuals and groups restructure their classroom delivery methods may be needed. Changing from traditional 45- to 55-minute periods to classroom sessions that are extended and/or shortened to vary time allotments creates the need for a variety of structural changes. These structural changes in class scheduling may, in turn, require that changes in areas such as administrative reporting procedures, job responsibilities, supervision schedules, and instructional technology requirements also be implemented. Bringing those responsible for implementation together to identify problems and needed supports and to coordinate tasks must be continuing activities.

Some forms of support must never be discontinued. They are required as long as the particular program, process, or project exists. On the other hand, others may be needed for only a short period of time. It is such variations in duration, intensity, content, focus, and form that reinforce the need for principals to have special knowledge and skills about supporting those responsible for implementation. Additionally, support may be needed at the individual, group, or organizational level, and sometimes at all three simultaneously. To provide a sampling of the kinds of knowledge and skills principals need in supporting those responsible for implementation, four areas of support are addressed in this chapter:

◆ effective staff development

◆ delegation

◆ reducing or removing organizational barriers

◆ modeling ongoing professional growth

These four areas represent only a starter list of knowledge and skills needed by principals if those responsible for implementation are to receive consistent and quality support in their efforts and accomplishments. However, working in these four areas will lead principals to other important areas. These four areas represent beginning points for principals in learning to provide support for those responsible for implementation.

EFFECTIVE STAFF DEVELOPMENT

Effective staff development is synonymous with supporting those responsible for implementation. If not, then "effective" is a questionable descriptor. In *The Principal as Staff Developer*, DuFour (1991) identified seven characteristics of effective staff development programs. He reported that effective staff development programs:

◆ are purposeful

◆ are designed to promote and influence teachers' thinking about teaching

◆ are research-based both in content and process

◆ have realistic time frames

◆ are evaluated at several different levels

◆ generate teacher commitment to the training

◆ have strong administrative support (pp. 56–70)

Given these seven characteristics, it should be obvious that effective staff development has matured far beyond the traditional, single-event inservice of the past. Even a cursory examination of the recent literature on staff development reveals the frequent use of such terms as job-embedded, systemic, life-long learning, learning communities, mentoring, school-based, context changes, continuous improvement, and quality. Dennis Sparks, Executive Director of the National Staff Development Council, identified eleven changes in both the definition and delivery of staff development. According to Sparks (1994, 1996), staff development has changed:

- *from* individual development *to* individual and organization development
- *from* fragmented, piecemeal improvement efforts *to* clear, coherent, planned programs
- *from* district-focused *to* school-focused
- *from* a focus on adult needs *to* a focus on student needs/learning outcomes
- *from* training away from the job *to* multiple-forms of job-embedded learning
- *from* an orientation toward the transmission of knowledge and skills *to* inquiry into the study of teaching and learning
- *from* a focus on generic instructional skills *to* a combination of generic and content-specific skills
- *from* staff developers as trainers *to* staff developers who consult, plan, and facilitate
- *from* staff development provided only by departments *to* staff development as a critical function performed by all administrators and teacher-leaders
- *from* teachers as the primary recipients *to* improved performance for everyone who affects student learning
- *from* staff development as a "frill" *to* staff development as an essential and indispensable process

According to Sparks (1994), these changes are the consequences of three powerful ideas:

- *Results-driven education* in which success is based on what students know and are able to do as a result of their time spent in school. This idea changes the way staff development is judged. Success of staff development is determined by its ability to change instructional behaviors that result in student benefits.

♦ *Systems thinking*, which involves a recognition of the complexity and interdependent nature of the various parts of a system. The application of this idea helps to give an wholistic view to the impact of various staff development efforts.

♦ *Constructivism*, which asserts that learners build their own knowledge structures rather than receive knowledge from a teacher. To become a constructivist teacher, individuals must be exposed to similar approaches in their own learning. Thus, collaboration, study groups, coaching, and other interactive approaches will be needed for the continued development of those responsible for implementation.

In elaborating on strong administrative support as a characteristic of effective staff development, DuFour and Berkey (1995) offered 10 suggestions to principals who want to develop their organizations through the professional development of their staff members:

♦ *Create* consensus on the school you are trying to become

♦ *Identify, promote, and protect* shared values

♦ *Monitor* the critical elements of the school improvement effort

♦ *Ensure* systematic collaboration throughout the school

♦ *Encourage* experimentation

♦ *Model* a commitment to professional growth

♦ *Provide* one-on-one staff development

♦ *Provide* staff development programs that are purposeful and research-based

- *Promote* individual and organization self efficacy
- *Stay* the course (pp. 3–5)

Many of these suggestions are similar to the knowledge and skills for successful implementation shared throughout this book. As you review DuFour and Berkey's list, recall earlier assertions that successful implementers need knowledge and skills in visioning; patience and persistence; monitoring; encouraging quality involvement; planning; leading through modeling; facilitation; and data-gathering and interpretation. Staff development activities provided at the right time and to the right persons is an important way for principals to support those responsible for implementation.

Knowing what support is needed, when, and by whom is an important skill for principals to develop. Processes that help principals identify what supports are needed were presented earlier. Among the most powerful for identifying needed supports are listening, questioning, and observing. Listening and questioning were presented as two of the areas in which principals need knowledge and skills. This is reasonable because facilitating is defined as "to make things easier" and making things easier is really what support for those responsible for implementation is intended to do. Additionally, all three of the processes (listening, questioning, and observing) are data-gathering mechanisms. The information generated from these can be sorted and framed through the use of one or more of the tools presented in Chapter 3.

Pankake and Palmer (1996) reviewed an example of using questioning, observing, and listening for data-gathering, and then sorting and framing the data for interpretation and action using the Stages of Concern Questionnaire as a tool. The data gathered and then profiled identified what concerns teachers experienced at various points in an effort to implement the inclusion of severely multiple-disabled students in regular kindergarten classrooms. The information regarding the teachers' concerns was then used to select the staff-development activities that would be most helpful to the teachers in supporting their implementation efforts. Different kinds of support were needed by different teachers, and even the same teacher needed different kinds of support at different points in the implementation process. Overall, Pankake and Palmer (1996) reported that staff development interventions need to be linked to the concerns teachers experience and they need to be immediately useful in continuing implementation efforts. Frequent use of the information-gathering processes (questioning, listening, and observing) and employment of the appropriate tools for analysis are invaluable to principals and those they need to support. Additionally, principals need to increase their awareness of the various forms that staff development can take in addressing the needs of those responsible for implementation.

The National Staff Development Council has long advocated staff-development models that include, but also go beyond, the typical "training" that we have all come to know as synonymous with staff development. Sparks and Loucks-Horsley (1990) reviewed five models of staff development. Each review included a definition, the assumptions underlying of the model, an overview of the model's theoretical foundation and related research, the major activity phases used in the model, and the results from using the model. These five models are representative of the variety of forms that effective staff development can take: individually guided staff development; observation/assessment; involvement in a development/improvement process; training; and inquiry. Effective staff development manifests itself as support for those responsible for implementation in a variety of forms.

Whether the implementation is of a routine activity, a new project, process or program or a unique event, support is a necessary condition in making it happen. The five models reviewed by Sparks and Loucks-Horsley (1990) include illustrations of how effective staff development can be embedded in implementation projects such as school development/improvement processes and action-research/study groups and in standard operational requirements in schools such as observations/assessments. Each of the five models exemplifies DuFour's (1991) seven characteristics of effective staff development programs. Each of the models reviewed by Sparks and Loucks-Horsley is purposeful, designed to promote and influence teachers' thinking about teaching, and is research-based. Additionally, the time frames for the models vary with what is realistic for the approach; each model can be evaluated from a variety of perspectives; all of the models are intended to generate teacher commitment to training; and all of the models require strong and persistent administrative support.

The five models also offer variety in terms of numbers involved (individuals, small groups, whole staff), focus (specific topic to organizational improvement), timing (single, short-term events to multiyear processes), levels of change required (creating new processes to improving existing processes), and learner investment (from use of existing knowledge to the development of new knowledge). The five models offered by the National Staff Development Council represent an excellent "starter set" for principals for developing knowledge and skills in the use of effective staff development as a means of supporting those responsible for implementation.

In the past, staff development has tended to be most abundant early in the change process. As districts and schools ready themselves for change, staff development sessions to provide general background about the innovation or new practice and the theory behind it are often plentiful. According to Joyce and Showers (1988), these theory and demonstration sessions are helpful in increasing awareness and providing information about the change but they result in little or no transfer to classroom practice. To be effective in supporting those responsible for implementation, staff development needs to go beyond informational/awareness level activities. This perspective regarding staff development aligns well with the focus of this book. That is, effective staff development must reflect the operational characteristics of a thoroughly planned and disciplined execution of a successful implementation project. Improved teaching and student learning are likely to follow.

DELEGATION

Implementation requires that numerous individuals operate simultaneously on a variety of activities to make things happen. A school cannot/will not stop operating while planning occurs; nor can it/will it stop in order for a new project, process, or procedure to be undertaken. New things must begin while other operations continue. Because so much must occur simultaneously, it is incumbent on the principal to become skilled in effective delegation. Delegating effectively can provide support for those responsible for implementation because it gives them autonomy and decision-making authority for their work. It is also a means for those responsible for implementation to provide support for the principal. When principals can empower others in the school to move ahead with efforts to implement, then they can use their knowledge and skills to coordinate, act as facilitators, provide feedback, assist in problem-solving, and engage in other leadership activities.

Yukl (1989) defines delegation as:

> The manager gives an individual or group the authority and responsibility for making a decision; the manager usually specifies limits within which the final choice must fall, and prior approval may or may not be required before a decision can be implemented (p. 84).

Given this definition, effective delegation is a necessary, but insufficient, condition for implementation. For "things to happen," groups and individuals must feel secure in making decisions. This feeling of security emanates from the principal giving *both* the authority and responsibility to do this. Without this, individuals and groups are left "running in place," waiting for directions from the principal before taking action. Anyone remotely familiar with a school can visualize what would happen (more appropriately, what would not happen) if this was standard operating procedure. Delegation is, if nothing else, a matter of self-preservation for principals. More importantly, it is a means of giving and demonstrating support for those responsible for implementation.

If delegation is to be effective, principals must observe certain requirements. Delegation doesn't just happen—it is led and managed. According to Krein (1982) many of us don't delegate enough, a few of us delegate too much, and most of us just don't delegate well. Knowing the characteristics of effective delegation, why it should be done and how it differs from ineffective delegation can provide a starting point for assessing our own knowledge and skills in delegation. Effective delegation requires communicating clearly, specifying authority, encouraging others' participation, reviewing results not methods, showing trust, giving support, being consistent. Those who delegate effectively allow others to make mistakes. Ineffective delegators, according to McConkey (1974), confuse responsibility and accountability, do not give or give only vague authority, provide inaccurate or inadequate data, create an atmosphere of fear so that others are afraid of making a wrong

decision, and do not set time limits. He asserted that learning
to delegate effectively is important because:

♦ It helps with *planning* because no one individual
  can know all of the details; involving several individuals in things can come close to having a group
  that knows all of the details.

♦ It helps in *controlling*, that is, in identifying who is
  accountable for what.

♦ *Evaluation* of performance can be based on the
  achievement or accomplishment of that which was
  delegated.

♦ It provides opportunities to *develop other people* in
  the organization by giving them practice in a variety of responsibilities.

♦ *Encouraging self-direction and motivation* in others is
  both empowering and *makes good use of the human
  resources* within the organization.

Effective delegation can be an important means for providing support for those responsible for implementation. The following are four forms of support that can be provided when
principals delegate effectively:

♦ Empowerment through limits

  When delegation is done effectively, it serves to foster the freedom of empowerment and the security
  of limitation. Waterman (1987) referred to this as direction and empowerment. Clear direction and setting of limits allows empowerment to occur. If principals have thought through and worked directly
  with others to define and clarify the direction, spec-
  ify the activities and sequence, communicate these
  elements clearly, and establish points for feedback
  (who, what, when, where, how, and to whom), then
  others can begin making thing happen. Within the
  set limits others can operate as needed and report
  progress or lack of it at the established feedback
  points. At these points, affirmation or adjustment

suggestions will occur in a spirit of improvement not reproach.

♦ Focus on accomplishments

Effective delegation requires telling an individual or group what needs to be accomplished, that is, what result or outcome is expected. In addition to identifying what must be accomplished, focus is given to what tasks and activities will be needed to get the desired results and who is responsible for making sure each task and activity is accomplished. Feedback will come in reports on progress being made toward the goal or objective to be accomplished.

♦ Provides a mechanism for effective communication

If delegation is to be effective, then the individual who is delegating a task and the individual(s) to whom the task is delegated must communicate regularly. Each of them must be able to both receive and give information in written and oral forms. Through the establishment of periodic feedback points, communication focused on progress toward the desired results occurs regularly. In addition to this vertical flow of information, increased communication with peers, that is, horizontal communication, is required to facilitate and coordinate tasks necessary to accomplish the objective.

♦ Provides a continuous energy source

Effective delegation can provide a continuous source of energy by motivating individuals through the establishment of challenging but achievable goals. Effective delegation is somewhat like the saying, "nothing succeeds like success." As individuals succeed with the tasks delegated to them, they become more confident and are inclined to seek additional responsibilities. Additionally, by sharing the necessary tasks among many

people the burden is distributed and the enthusiasm and energy are multiplied.

Developing skills in effective delegation can be a way for
principals to provide support to those responsible for implementation. By empowering others, focusing on accomplishments, creating channels for communication, and generating
synergy through group efforts, principals create conditions
that are more likely to allow successful implementation to
occur.

REDUCING OR REMOVING ORGANIZATIONAL BARRIERS

Sometimes the greatest support principals can provide to
those responsible for implementation is to eliminate something. It is often the case that as change occurs more changes
are required. The implementation of new programs or major
changes in existing ones will most likely require adjustments in
other areas of school operations. Skill in identifying organizational barriers that need to be reduced or removed in order to
support the implementation of new efforts is one that principals should seek to develop. Once the barriers are identified,
principals must also be able to take actions that cause their reduction and/or elimination. The following are some organizational issues that can present difficulties for those responsible
for implementation. Each issue is followed by recommended
action(s) for reducing or removing the difficulties this issue
generates.

ISSUE: *Poor delegation.* Springboarding from the previous discussion, it is important for principals to realize that more or less effective delegation can be either a support or a barrier to those responsible for
implementation. Those responsible for implementation need to be clear about when the choice is theirs
to make. If empowerment is merely a popular term
to use rather than a real framework for operating,
then confusion will occur. Individuals and groups
generate a lack of trust when they are told, "It's up
to you," "Do what you think is best," or "Take the

ball and run with it," and when they do, they are chastised or even usurped in their decisions.

ACTION: Be clear in defining who is responsible for what. This is not only critical for the principal and those being empowered, it is also essential for those who will be affected by these decisions. Delegating authority and responsibility to others is an important organizational issue that must be addressed if successful implementation is to occur. When this has been done well, individuals and groups will proceed with confidence. Additionally, those affected by the decisions will not be questioning—"Can they do that?," "Who put him in charge of that?," or "I'm not doing that until someone in authority tells me I have to." Everyone should be clear on who can make and implement what decisions. Doing this requires effective delegation, communication, and leadership skills from the principal.

ISSUE: *Activity Overload.* This occurs when too much is going on at the same time and people are becoming overwhelmed. When project after project is initiated, it is difficult to tell which (if any) is truly important to pursue. When everything becomes a priority and is said to deserve our time and attention, the result is usually none of them become our priority and none receive our attention. Chronic instances of this result in a "this too shall pass" behavior or "don't worry about it, it's just this year's new thing." No one worries about or pays attention to new projects, procedures, or processes because soon a whole new set will be presented and those being celebrated today will soon be yesterday's news. In *Change and Technology Leadership* (Pankake, 1996), the point was made that change agents are often frustrated when others show resistance to proposed changes. However, what these individuals may be resisting is not the basic intent of the change, but the consequences of pursuing it. Ignoring any new activities becomes a means of survival.

ACTION: Knowing when too many things are underway and that introducing more will likely result in less is a sensitivity that principals must develop if successful implementation is to occur. First, principals should watch carefully to see when "overload" is happening. If overload does occur pause or take a breather for a time while things settle a bit. Or, say "no" or " not just yet" to new proposals. Another strategy is to stop doing some things, that is, explore what practices or projects should be given up and focus attention on the program, projects, and processes that are important. Others will do the same. If principals pay attention to a program, process or project, so will everyone else; likewise what they pay less attention to will also receive less attention from others.

ISSUE: *Working at Cross-purposes.* This happens when existing projects, procedures, processes, and structures conflict with or are deterrents to making the desired activities of new initiatives happen. Some common examples of this include:

- trying to implement a performance-based or portfolio system to assess student learning but retaining the standard letter grading and report card systems
- advocating an integrated curriculum but retaining content-specific testing
- encouraging a variety of means for professional growth opportunities but rewarding only formal graduate credit options
- setting the use of technology as a priority and then limiting access to equipment with elaborate "checkout" procedures and restricted use schedules

Hundreds of examples can be found in every organization.

ACTION: Be open to hearing about such situations whether they relate to instructional issues, administrative procedures, or support services. Another proactive measure is to do an analysis of the environment to determine if some problem that exists there is "working at cross-purposes," that is, is preventing the desired behavior and perhaps even rewarding the undesired behavior. A third option to consider is using some of the tools from Chapter 3 to reveal the environmental conditions preventing full implementation.

ISSUE: *Standardization.* This involves treating everyone the same. However, in our efforts to be fair, we often create conditions that increase unfairness. By doing such things as making everyone attend the same training, allocating resources equally to each participant, and providing the same number of feedback opportunities to those involved, support takes on a standardization that may do as much damage as good. Individual differences and specific situations deserve to be handled in such a way that performance is maximized. Providing "supports" that do not address the specific needs of an individual or situation may be the same as providing no support at all.

ACTION: Use tools such as the Stages of Concern Questionnaire and the affinity diagram to identify individual needs. These instruments and the information they provide can be critical in helping principals tailor the types of supports offered. Empower implementers with opportunities to make adjustments that best fit their circumstances. The limits to such adjustments can easily be established by defining the parameters within which the implementers must operate and the performance levels they are expected to maintain. Encourage variations in approaches by establishing pilot programs with appropriate summative evaluations to determine effectiveness of each.

ISSUE: *Tradition.* Some activities and procedures in an organization are done because they always have been, that is, they are traditional. These activities and procedures may or may not be effective; they merely continue unevaluated. While some of these traditions are important to the creation and maintenance of the organizational culture, others might best be stopped and the resources reallocated to more productive efforts. Organizational culture components are likely to have strong advocacy and protection. Care should be taken in assessing which traditions are the organizational culture components and which are merely those about which can be said, "we've always done it this way."

ACTION: Spend time acquainting yourself with why certain procedures and activities in the organization are done. Ask questions about these procedures of a variety of organizational members; be sure that various organizational roles and perspectives are represented. Honor those activities and procedures that are organizational culture components, while slowly abandoning unproductive activities or procedures, and initiating new ones. As these efforts get underway, it is important that principals not replace one unproductive activity or procedure with another. Be sure to include an evaluation component for each new initiative to assure that an increase in productivity has been achieved. Because traditions are important to organizational culture and the institutionalization of new programs, projects, and processes, principals should create new traditions that help support the continuation of the practices needed for successful implementation of these efforts.

ISSUE: *Bureaucratic Frustration.* Efforts to restructure schools and school districts have been emphasized in the last decade; however, bureaucratic elements still characterize most educational organizations. The multiple layers of the bureaucracy with approval or veto powers, the disconnectedness often found between and among the various specialized units within the bureaucracy, and the numerous rules and regulations ("red tape") that often operate in conflict with each other, can cause frustration to all but the most persistent and patient among us. The frequency and intensity of this frustration with the bureaucracy results in delays, false starts, halts, and termination of implementation efforts. This frustration may even prevent some innovations from being suggested for consideration.

ACTION: Do as much up-front communication and coordination as possible to reduce the delays at critical points. Regular progress reports that include statements of future needs and anticipated actions can help keep various individuals informed and reduce the amount of time needed to process requests. Start early when you know that something needs to work its way up through the system. If it takes 30 days to move from building to school board, don't wait until 10 days before you need it to initiate the request. Invite representatives of various specialized units to serve on project planning and/or evaluation committees. This helps secure their involvement, cooperation, and perhaps even coordination with other units. Use your patience and persistence and encourage these characteristics in others on your staff. Progress, while slow, is still progress; and slow, steady progress in implementing effective programs, projects, and processes is certainly preferable to "wishful thinking" or references to "we tried that once, but it didn't work."

ISSUE: *No Time To....* It seems no matter what the situation, there is never enough time to accomplish everything desired. This is even more pronounced in schools when so many of the necessary activities have fixed time parameters. Finding time for collaboration, scheduling meetings to create involvement without creating burdens, finding time for both basic instruction and enrichment activities, allowing time for paperwork without letting paperwork become time-consuming, and myriad other issues of "no time to..." make up one of the most frequently voiced categories of needed support for implementation. Because time is a finite resource, principals can't "create time." They can, however, make the best use of the time available.

ACTION: Examine existing schedules to be sure that the best and most efficient use of facilities and personnel is happening. Invite a variety of individuals to search the existing schedule for possible improvements; multiple perspectives can often find possibilities that have been overlooked. Of course, if areas for improvement are identified, changes should be pursued. Try to schedule project teams and committee members in such a way that they have some common planning time for their meetings. Even if this can't be done all of the time, being able to provide this time periodically may well increase individuals' willingness to volunteer some of their own time for the same purpose. Realize that there isn't enough time for everything and then prioritize activities, select new initiatives carefully, and distribute involvement so that no one person or group is overburdened.

The organizational barriers reviewed here are only a few from among the many that exist in schools and school districts everywhere. Begin with these in analyzing the situation in your school or school district. However, be open to looking for others that are not listed here. Principals need to become knowledgeable about organizational barriers; additionally, they need to become skilled in the identification and application of actions to reduce or remove these barriers. Further, it is important that they also realize that some organizational barriers can be neither reduced nor removed. When this happens, principals need to recognize the intractability of the situation and move on to work in those areas where changes can be made.

MODELING ONGOING PROFESSIONAL GROWTH

The terms "life-long learner" and "learning community" have found their way into most conversations dealing with schools and school improvement efforts. There is a desire to assure that schools operate as learning communities and that both the students and the professionals who people them operate as life-long learners. Senge's *The Fifth Discipline* (1990) has become one of the most referenced works in recent years. Talking and writing about life-long learning and learning communities are easier than operationalizing them. Yet, if we are to believe the power claimed for these concepts in influencing both the individuals and organizations within which we work, then we must persist in trying to implement these concepts in the daily routines of schools. If this is to happen, principals will be key facilitators. Principals must model the important knowledge and skills needed to make the concepts of life-long learner and learning community realities in practice.

Of the types of support that need to be provided to those responsible for seeing that implementation occurs, this modeling of ongoing professional growth of self and the organization may well be the most important. Ongoing professional growth efforts are the means through which other supports are realized. Certainly, staff development becomes increasingly effective when it is based on individual needs and those determined as necessary for development of the organization. As the organization and the individuals within it mature, delegation becomes more prominent, inclusive, and effective. And as the organization learns from itself, measures that adjust internal operations in such ways that barriers to achieving desired results are reduced or removed altogether will naturally follow. Life-long learning for individuals and an organization that operates as a learning community enable other necessary supports to evolve. Principals need to gain the knowledge and skills to move themselves, their colleagues, and their organizations to full operations in these states of growth. The following are 10 suggested actions that principals can take in helping assure ongoing professional growth of themselves and others:

- Be the lead learner!

  Principals must model the behavior they wish to see in others. If principals want faculty members to be excited about acquiring new knowledge and skills, they must demonstrate their own excitement for acquiring new knowledge and skills. Without question, staff, students, colleagues, supervisors, parents, and community must view the principal as the "lead learner," the one who sets the pace and standard for all to follow. Principals must be the leaders in life-long learning if they truly believe it is important. They must go beyond exhortations. They must take the lead in blazing the learning trail. As Bennis (1989) noted, "Leadership is first being , then doing. Everything the leader does reflects what he or she is" (p. 141). If principals want life-long learners, they first need to be life-long learners.

- Share what you have learned!

  Learning is a very social enterprise. To read, hear, or experience something individually only marks the first level of learning. It is when we have the opportunity to talk about it and listen to the related experiences of others that learning begins to truly become a part of us. Principals need to be proactive in sharing what they have learned with others. Conversations, demonstrations, study groups, electronic chat groups, informal visits, and any other opportunities to share ideas, questions, comments, and concerns with others should be taken as often as possible. Attending workshops with others, reading books as a part of group study, and scheduling time for feedback following demonstrations and implementation efforts are all ways to assure that the social element of learning is in place.

♦ Make learning available!

Principals need to be proactive in encouraging learning for self and others. One way to do this is to make opportunities to learn available constantly. This may be done by setting aside resources specifically for attending workshops and conferences, or by inviting presenters to the school. It might be done by making professional library resources with journals, books, and newsletters from a variety of professional associations made available to staff; it might be done electronically, by providing Internet access to students and staff to engage in conversations with others who know about or are also interested in learning about specific topics. And it can be done by instituting study groups and action research groups on particular topics of interest. These are only a few of the ways learning can be made available in an organization. The means are limited only by the creativity of those in the organization. Principals can initiate some opportunities; then principals should stand back and lend their support to the creative ideas for making learning available in the organization that will be generated by the staff and students, themselves.

♦ Encourage it!

Just making learning available won't suffice. Principals must also encourage individuals to take advantage of the opportunities presented. One way this occurs is for principals to practice their "lead learner" behaviors and model taking advantage of available opportunities. Another way is for principals to use their skills in questioning to ask those who do access the opportunities what they have learned, how they are using what they learned, and what new things they plan to learn next. A third way for principals to encourage learning in their organizations is to make taking advantage of learning opportunities easy. If it requires "an act of Congress" to secure travel funds, or to order a

book, or to get copies of materials to distribute, individuals will soon be discouraged rather than encouraged. Help encourage learning in your organization by making access to learning as easy as
possible.

♦ Reward it!

Recognition can be a powerful reinforcement for
desired behavior. If principals want individuals in
their organizations to become life-long learners
then they need to develop ways to reward individuals who pursue learning. Recognition might
come in a number of forms, such as appointment as
study group leader for a particular topic; opportunity to conduct staff development sessions; mem-
bership in a related professional association or sub-
scription to a related journal; selection to serve as
organizational representative on various district
and community committees and task forces; relief
from some committees and/or teaching responsibilities to pursue learning opportunities; salary increases or other monetary rewards; or scholarships
or letters of commendation. Recall the importance
of monitoring (paying attention) in successful implementation. If principals desire that life-long
learning be implemented in their schools, then
monitoring it via rewards for those who practice it
will aid in making it a reality.

♦ Reflect, Process and Connect!

"Reflection is a major way in which leaders learn
from the past " (Bennis, 1989, p. 114). In the busy
world of operating schools, time for reflection is
scarce. However, because reflection is an important
mechanism for learning, principals need to make
time for reflection for themselves, their professional colleagues and students. Practicing thinking
about what we have learned, using it to analyze the
past, and identifying ways to improve future performance signals that important learning is occurring. Learning evidences itself in behavior changes.

Bennis and Nanus (1985) defined organizational learning as "the process by which an organization obtains and uses new knowledge, tools, behaviors, and values" (p. 191). This is no less true for the individual. Reflection, processing of new information, and connecting new knowledge to existing knowledge are important elements of life-long learning strategies for individuals and organizations.

♦ Start with "I don't know!"

The path to life-long learning begins with a declaration that there are things that need to be learned. No one person can know everything; there is always something else to learn. With the knowledge explosion in today's world, all professionals must commit themselves to learning for survival in this era of rapid change. However, if an individual really believes they already know all that is important to know, life-long learning is over before it has begun. If the "lead learner" is unable to utter "I don't know" and then proceed to do something to correct it, how can anyone else in the organization be admonished to act differently? If, as Bennis and Nanus (1985) say, "This quality of fostering organizational learning by example may be one of the most important functions of leadership" (p. 205), then the flood-gates to learning must be opened by a simple act of leadership, that is, leading by example.

♦ Learn by design and learn at the moment!

Some learning should be purposeful and planned. Other learning should be impromptu. It is impossible to know everything you are going to need to know, and therefore impossible to plan all of your learning. Certainly we can choose the things that we want to learn and plan the activities in which we will engage in learning it. However, we must also be alert to the learning opportunities that come to us at the moment. This learning is unplanned and often offered through chance. Unplanned learning

might come to us through a conversation with a colleague, a program on television or radio, a problem
in need of solving, a need expressed by a child, or
listening to the words of a song, poem, or story.
Learning at the moment may add to what we are
learning by design or even cause us to change the
design to accommodate this new interest. Being
proactive by planning some of what we want to
learn and how we will accomplish it is important;
but, equally important is to stay open to new opportunities to learn as they present themselves.
Principals need to develop an approach to learning
that is both purposeful (by design) and flexible (at
the moment).

♦ Create new knowledge!

Schools are important laboratories where existing
knowledge can be applied and new knowledge can
be created. Various forms of action research, study
groups, and evaluation projects can be used to systematically apply and evaluate recommended
ideas and practices. Additionally, learning organizations will formulate their own hypotheses and
evaluate them against the results they generate in
practice. This new knowledge in turn can be offered as recommended ideas and practices for others to apply and evaluate in their own settings.
Thus, the link between knowledge production and
knowledge utilization is strengthened. Even the
process of creating new knowledge is itself a
source of learning for the organization and the people in it.

♦ Be inclusive!

It should be next to impossible for principals to
identify something about which they do not wish to
learn. Principals should look everywhere for opportunities to learn—in the field of education, in business, science, literature, economics, music, technology, and so forth. There really is not a subject or
issue that cannot be important to our personal or

professional development in some way. Repeatedly, issues and areas that seemed unrelated to educators' personal and professional lives at one point have at another point developed into essential areas of knowledge and skills for success. Principals must not exclude any topic or type of learning. They must use every means available to learn and aid others in their learning. Life-long learners and members of learning communities need to be inclusive about what they learn and the means they use to learn.

In *Leading Change*, Kotter (1996) identified five mental habits that support life-long learning: risk taking, humble self-reflection, solicitation of opinions, careful listening, and openness to new ideas. These habits echo the concepts presented here. Principals must commit themselves to these habits and implement the suggested actions if they are to exemplify life-long learning and transform their schools to learning communities. DuFour (1991) summarizes this important role stating: "Principals who recognize that school improvement means people improvement and commit themselves to creating conditions to promote the professional growth of their teachers, can make an enormous difference in their schools" (p. 96).

SUMMARY

Supporting those responsible for implementation is essential if success is to be achieved. The support provided must be continuous, must come in a variety of forms, and must meet the needs of the user. This chapter presented four categories of support important to those responsible for implementation. They are by no means the only kinds of support that can and must be provided for implementation efforts to succeed. Principals can begin with these, but are encouraged to use their skills in questioning, listening, data analysis, and judgment to generate information useful in determining support needs. The most important point for principals to keep in mind is that support for those responsible for implementation is a must. While the form, intensity, and type of support may vary, the fact that those responsible for implementation have a need to be supported in their efforts will not.

FOLLOW-UP ACTIVITIES

1. Secure a copy of the *Standards for Staff Development* (1995) from the National Staff Development Council. (Elementary, Middle, and High School editions are available.) Administer and score the "Self-Assessment and Planning Tool" at the end of the document. Use the results of this assessment as a catalyst for staff discussions regarding staff development as a means for supporting those responsible for implementation. Identify areas of strength and need; implement maintenance and improvement activities.

2. Use the 10 suggested actions to help assure the ongoing professional growth of self and others to create a diagnostic instrument regarding your performance in this area of support. For example, list each of the suggested behaviors and then provide a Likert Scale for evaluating the performance level:

	Never			Always	
I model the learning behavior I desire from others.	1	2	3	4	5
I share what I have learned.	1	2	3	4	5
I make learning available.	1	2	3	4	5

Administer the instrument to yourself and ask three to five other trusted colleague to complete it as well. Use the data to diagnose your professional growth actions and develop plans to maintain and/or improve these behaviors as appropriate. You might also ask the staff to do the same procedure in relationship to their modeling of professional growth (life-long learning) with students.

3. Create a "Demolition Crew" (made up of staff, central office representatives, community representatives, and perhaps even some students) to identify organizational barriers that may be stalling various implementation projects and to generate possible actions to take in reducing or removing these barriers.

7

CLOSING WITH A FEW BRIEF REFLECTIONS

At the beginning of this book, the image of a riverbed for the "converging streams of behavior" was offered as a means of describing implementation in relationship to the other 20 knowledge and skill domains identified by the National Policy Board for Educational Administration. The information presented in the preceding chapters was intended to elaborate on this image. Additionally, at this stage, no justification should be needed to gain agreement that implementation is appropriately classified as one of the "Functional Domains," that is, one of those that "address the organizational processes and techniques by which the mission of the school is achieved. They provide for the educational program to be realized and allow the institution to function" (National Commission for the Principalship, 1990, p. 21). Throughout this book, emphasis was given to describing successful implementation as possible, though certainly not easy. Every chapter offered information important and useful to anyone seeking to increase their knowledge and skills regarding successful implementation. The intended messages from each of the chapters are distilled in the five recommended behaviors that follow. Each of these behaviors requires a great deal of knowledge and many skills. Still, they point to the places to start for those interested in successful implementation.

♦ Take action

Implementation means "making things happen. Readiness is important, action is a requirement. Even if the first actions aren't 100% correct, at least things are underway. *Once started, improvements can be made.*

◆ Review and preview

If implementation is to succeed, simultaneous looks backward and forward are required. Where have we been; what have we done; what can be improved? Where are we headed; what new things do we need; how can we make it happen? Reviewing and previewing help form a sturdy loop or link that takes the best from the past and sustains it, while simultaneously taking on new initiatives to replace what can be better. Like a mountain road, straight up is impossible; but to move in a spiraling pattern assures steady progress and ultimate success.

◆ Facilitate the people and the process

Skilled facilitation may be among the most important things that principals can do to assure successful implementation. Making things easier is what skilled facilitators do. Coordinating tasks and encouraging the collaboration between and among those involved are ways to make things easier.

◆ Pay attention

Nothing runs on automatic pilot forever. Monitoring must be done if successful implementation is to be sustained. Monitoring must be done in a variety of ways and by a variety of individuals. The important point is that it must be done. Check out any processes, projects, or programs that are being successfully implemented and you will find that there is someone paying attention to (monitoring) the implementation.

◆ Provide support in all its forms

Successful implementation is not a single occurrence, but rather a continuous stream of activities. Support of various kinds are needed to get things going and to keep things going. The kinds of support may vary but the need for support does not. Principals must be supportive and provide supports if successful implementation is to be sustained.

Becoming knowledgeable and skilled in the implementation domain requires all that is presented in this volume and more. Using the 10 suggested actions that principals can take to help assure the ongoing professional growth of themselves and others offered in Chapter Six is an excellent place to begin this development. The important thing is to begin; make things happen—implement!

REFERENCES

American Heritage Dictionary (Second College Edition) (1982). Boston, MA: Houghton Mifflin Co.

Archer, P. (1994). *Benchmarking plus: A strategic imperative*. Workshop presented at the Total Quality Forum VI: Meet the Challenge–Lead the Change, October 18–21, 1994, Dallas, TX.

ASCD's Research Information Service (1982). Highlights from research on effective school leadership. *Educational Leadership*, 39(5), 349.

Benjamin, R. (1981). *Making schools work: A reporter's journey through some of America's most remarkable classrooms*. New York: Continuum.

Bennis, W. & Nanus, B. (1985). *Leaders: The strategies for taking charge*. New York, NY: Harper & Row.

Bennis, W. (1989). *On becoming a leader*. Reading, MA: Addison-Wesley.

Bone, D. (1988). *The business of listening: A practical guide to effective listening*. Menlo Park, CA: Crisp.

Bridges, W. (1991). *Managing transitions: Making the most of change*. Reading, MA: Addison Wesley.

Camp, R.C. (1989). *Benchmarking: The search for industry best practices that lead to superior performance*. Milwaukee, WI: ASQC Quality Press.

Conner, D.R. (1993). *Managing at the speed of change: How resilient managers succeed and prosper where others fail*. New York: Villard Books.

Covey, S.R. (1989). *The 7 habits of highly effective people: Powerful lessons in personal change*. New York, NY: Fireside Books.

Cuban, L. (1990). Reforming again, again, and again. *Educational Researcher*. 19(1), 3–13.

Drucker, P.F. (1954). *The practice of management: A study of the most important function in American society.* New York: Harper & Row.

DuFour, R.P (1991). *The principal as staff developer.* Bloomington, IN: National Educational Service.

DuFour, R. & Berkey, T. (1995). The principal as staff developer. *Journal of Staff Development, 16*(4), 2–6.

DuFour, R. & Eaker, R. (1992). *Creating the new American school: A principal's guide to school improvement.* Bloomington, IN: National Education Service.

DuPont de Nemours and Company (1989). *Leadership development process.* Austin, TX: The Texas LEAD Center.

Erlandson, D.A. (1980). An organizing strategy for managing change in the school. *NASSP Bulletin, 64*(435), 1–8.

Erlandson, D.A. (1997). *Organizational oversight: Planning and scheduling for effectiveness.* Larchmont, NY: Eye on Education.

Fullan, M.G. & Hargreaves, A. (1991). *What's worth fighting for? Working together for your school.* Toronto, ON: Ontario Public School Teachers' Federation.

Fullan, M.G., with Stiegelbauer, S. (1991). *The new meaning of educational change* (2nd ed.). New York: Teachers College Press.

Fullan, M.G. & Miles, M.B. (1992). Getting reform right: What works and what doesn't. *Phi Delta Kappan, 73*(10), 745–52.

Guskey, T.R. (1985). *Implementing mastery learning.* Belmont, CA: Wadsworth.

Guskey, T.R. (1995). Professional development in education: In search of the optimal mix. In T.R. Guskey & M. Huberman (Eds.). *Professional Development in Education: New Paradigms and Practices.* New York: Columbia Teachers College Press (114–31).

Hall, G.E., Newlove, B.W., George, A.A., Rutherford, W.L. & Hord, S.M. (1991). *Measuring change facilitator stages of concern: A manual for use of the CFSoC Questionnaire.* Greeley, CO: Center for Research on Teaching and Learning, University of Northern Colorado.

Hamilton, C. with Parker, C. (1993). *Communicating for results.* Belmont, CA: Wadsworth.

Hanson, E.M. (1991). *Educational administration and organizational behavior* (3rd ed.). Boston: Allyn and Bacon.

Harvey, T.L. (1990). *Checklist for change: A pragmatic approach to creating and controlling change.* Boston: Allyn and Bacon.

Hord, S.M., Rutherford, W.L., Huling-Austin, L., & Hall, G.E. (1987). *Taking charge of change.* Alexandria, VA: Association for Supervision and Curriculum Development.

Hoy, W.K. & Miskel, C.G. (1996). *Educational administration: Theory, research and practice* (5th ed.). New York: McGraw-Hill, Inc.

Hunsaker, R.A. (1983). *Understanding & developing the skills of oral communication: Speaking & listening.* Englewood, CO: Morton.

Hunter, M. (1982). *Mastery teaching.* El Segundo, CA: TIP Publications.

Hyerle, D. (1996). *Visual tools for constructing knowledge.* Alexandria, VA: Association for Supervision and Curriculum Development.

Joyce, B. & Showers, B. (1988). *Student achievement through staff development.* New York: Longman.

Kanter, R.B. , Stein, B.A. & Jick, T.D. (1992). *The challenge of organizational change: How companies experience it and leaders guide it.* New York: The Free Press.

Kirby, P.G. (1980, August). Quality decisions start with good questions. *Supervisory Management,* 2–7.

Kotter, J.P. (1996). *Leading change.* Boston, MA: Harvard Business School Press.

Kouzes, J.M. & Posner, B.Z. (1987). *The leadership challenge: How to get extraordinary things done in organizations.* San Francisco, CA: Jossey-Bass.

Krein, T.J. (1982). How to improve delegation habits. *Management Review,* 71(5), 58–61.

Lakein, A. (1973). *How to get control of your time and your life.* New York: The New American Library.

Lewis, J.P. (1991). *Project planning, scheduling and control: A hands-on guide to bringing projects in on time and on budget.* Chicago, IL: Probus.

Lewis, R.G. & Smith, D.H. (1994). *Total quality in higher education.* Delray Beach, FL: St. Lucie Press.

Lippitt, G.L., Langseth, P. & Mossop, J. (1985). *Implementing organizational change.* San Francisco: Jossey-Bass.

Lunenburg, F.C. & Ornstein, A.C. (1996). *Educational administration: Concepts and practices* (2nd ed.). Belmont, CA: Wadsworth.

Mager, R.F. , & Pipe, P. (1970). *Analyzing performance problems or "you really oughta wanna."* Belmont, CA: Pitman Learning.

Mager, R.F. & Pipe, P. (1984). *Analyzing performance problems or "you really oughta wanna"* (2nd ed.). Belmont CA: Pitman Learning.

Martin, T.L., Jr. (1973). *Malice in blunderland.* New York: McGraw-Hill.

McConkey, D.D. (1974). *No-nonsense delegation.* New York: Amacom.

McConkey, D.D. (1983). *How to manage by results* (4th ed.). New York: Amacom.

McLaughlin, J.A. (1990). *A guide for planning and conducting an evaluation of local special education programs.* Topeka, KS: Kansas State Department of Education, Special Education Administration Section.

National Commission for the Principalship (1990). *Principals for our changing schools: Preparation and certification.* Fairfax, VA: author.

National Policy Board for Educational Administration (NPBEA) (1993). *Principals for our changing schools: Knowledge and skill base.* Fairfax, VA: author.

National Staff Development Council (1995). *Standards for staff development.* Oxford, OH: author.

Pankake, A.M. (1986–87). A trip toward excellence. *National Forum of Educational Administration and Supervision Journal, 3*(3), 161–65.

Pankake, A.M. (1996). Change and technology leadership: Two sides of the same coin. *Educational Considerations*, 23(2), 25–28.

Pankake, A.M. & Burnett, I.E. (1990). *The effective elementary school principal*. Palm Springs, CA: ETC.

Pankake, A.M. & Palmer, B. (1996). Making the connections: Linking staff development interventions to implementation of full inclusion. *Journal of Staff Development*, 17(3), 26–30.

Popham, W.J. (1990). *Modern educational measurement: A practitioner's perspective* (2nd ed.). Englewood Cliffs, NJ: Prentice Hall.

Pryor, M.G., Pankake, A., & Hoskison, S. (1995). *Benchmarking*. Commerce, TX: Center for Excellence.

Quaglia, R. J. (1991). The nature of change. *Journal of Maine Education*, 7(1), 13–16.

Quick, T.L. (1992). *Successful team building*. New York: Amacom.

Roberts, W. (1987). *Leadership secrets of Attila the Hun*. New York: Warner Books.

Sandy, W. (1991). Avoid the breakdown between planning and implementation. *The Journal of Business Strategy*, 12(5), 30–33.

Senge, P.M. (1990). *The fifth discipline: The art & practice of the learning organization*. New York: Doubleday Currency.

Shelley, B. (1995). Facilitator presentation at the East Texas State University, Administrative Planning Retreat, September 18–19, 1995, at Tanglewood Resort and Conference Center, Pottsboro, TX.

Shiba, S. Graham, A. & Walden, D. (1993). *A new American TQM: Four practical revolutions in management*. Portland, OR: Productivity Press.

Southwest Educational Development Laboratory (n.d.). *Leadership for change*. Austin, TX: Author.

Southwest Educational Development Laboratory (n.d.). *Leadership for change II*. Austin, TX: Author.

Sparks, D. (1994). A paradigm shift in staff development. *Journal of Staff Development*, 15(4), 26–29.

Sparks, D. (1996). Paradigm shift in staff development. Presentation given at the National Staff Development Council's Academy VII, June 1996 at McDonald's Corporation Headquarters, Oakbrook, IL.

Sparks, D. & Loucks-Horsley, S. (1990). *Five models of staff development for teachers.* Oxford, OH: National Staff Development Council.

Texas Instruments Human Resources Development Defense Systems and Electronics Groups (1992). *Process flow charting self-paced course for teams.* Dallas, TX: Author.

Texas Instruments Defense Systems and Electronics Groups (7/1992). *Total Quality: Business Process Management (Adapted from Business Process Analysis, by Peter Walker. TIL.).* Dallas, TX: Author.

Todnem, G. & Warner, M.P. (1994). Demonstrating the benefits of staff development: An interview with Thomas R. Guskey. *Journal of Staff Development,* 15(3), 63–64.

Tucker, M.W. & Davis, D.A. (1994). Key ingredients for successful implementation of just-in-time: A system for all business sizes. *Business Horizons* (May-June), 59–65.

Tuckman, B.W. (1985). *Evaluating instructional programs* (2nd ed.). Boston: Allyn and Bacon.

Walton, M. (1986). *The Deming management method.* New York: Perigee Books.

Waterman, R.H., Jr. (1987). *The renewal factor: How the best get and keep the competitive edge.* New York: Bantam Books.

Whitaker, K.S. & Moses, M.C. (1994). *The restructuring handbook: A guide to school revitalization.* Boston: Allyn and Bacon.

Yukl, G.A. (1989). *Leadership in organizations* (2nd ed.). Englewood Cliffs, NJ: Prentice Hall.